Jolly Humor To Tickle Your Funny Bone

Buddy Webb

authorHOUSE

AuthorHouse™
1663 Liberty Drive
Bloomington, IN 47403
www.authorhouse.com
Phone: 1 (800) 839-8640

Published by AuthorHouse   03/30/2017

ISBN: 978-1-5246-8490-7 (sc)
ISBN: 978-1-5246-8489-1 (e)

Library of Congress Control Number: 2017904462

Print information available on the last page.

Dedication

TO THE SPIRIT OF PETER PAN WHO

WATCHES OVER EVERY LOVING FAMILY WITH CARE

Introduction

I owe my love of writing to the positive experience I got from joining a writing group in the St. Louis area.

It was composed of a variety of people with various interests. We met every Wednesday and shared our latest efforts.

Some wrote pieces about nature. Others were into short stories. Others were into expressing their feelings about serious topics. I wrote a variety of pieces about humorous and serious topics.

Various forms of writing were used—plays, essays, poems and dialogues.

This book contains the best humorous pieces that I wrote. Members of the writing group really liked them—they smiled, laughed and giggled

I hope that they will tickle your funny bone. Laughter is good for your soul and body. Even doctors agree to that.

To add to your enjoyment, I include sketches of odd looking characters who recite a silly limerick to give you a giggle.

So, now sit back, read and enjoy!

List of Funny Pieces

LiMERicks

BY

My Beloved Raytonia

I'm going to tell you a secret that you may find hard to believe. I swear by all that is holy that it is true. I feel that I must tell someone and—I know I can trust you to keep my secret. Well, here it is—my secret. I'm married to a woman from Jupiter. Yes, my wife Louise— actually her name is *@&%#—pronounced Ā À Kả Nả and translated "Raytonia"—is a Jupiterian.

When I was dating my wife, she did not tell me that she came from another planet. Of course, she always seemed so mysterious to me. At the time I thought that it was one of her more attractive qualities. I remember asking to meet her parents on several occasions and she told me that a meeting would be difficult because they had "gone on holiday on a ship." Of course, she never told me that it was a space ship. I never did meet them which looking back should have told me something. Later, my wife told me that she didn't tell me that she was a Jupiterian because she felt—and I totally agree—that I would have dropped her like a hot comet and written her off as a spaced-out weirdo.

Even I didn't suspect her origin until after we had been married for many years. By that time she could no longer hide the effects of living on Earth. As Jupiterians age it is more difficult for them to deal with Earth's impact on their bodies. Their ability to transform themselves to look like those around them is affected. They slowly start going back to their original form which according to Raytonia is something like the Pillsbury doughboy.

When these changes started occurring, Louise or should I say Raytonia felt compelled to tell me about how she had arrived on Earth in a space ship in 1939. It was one of those flying saucers that one hears and reads about. Anyway, it crashed landed and the crew members were forced to make their home on planet Earth. She operated the memory bank on board the craft. She said that she was quite good at it and was looking forward to a long career in the Jupiter Outer Space Agency.

The Jupiterian body is not up to receiving the great amounts of fat, salt and sugar found in an Earthling's daily diet. In her case the situation was made worse by the fact that she lived in the United States which is notorious in the galaxy for its terrible unhealthy fast-food. She often laments, "If only I crashed landed in Tibet, I would probably be healthier today."

One thing that gets worse over the years is eyesight. Jupiterian eyes are damaged by the high content of sugar in the diet. My wife has always worn special glasses but lately her eyesight has become weaker so she now must wear a set of binuculars afixed to eyeglass frames. She looks a bit peculiar because the binuculars stick out about three inches. It gives her a "beyond our planet" look.

Another thing that changes over time in a Jupiterian body is the make up of the blood or @#x3—pronounced. Ā Kōō and translated "jup juice." It becomes very thin so that special injections of @#x3$ pronounced Ā Kōō Tà and translated "jup juice plus" must be taken in the morning and evening in order to restore the consistency of the "jup juice."

Another thing that is affected is a sense of balance. Earth's gravity is weaker than that found on Jupiter. Over the years the Jupiterian's aging body can't adjust to the difference and his/her mobility is affected. Stairs become a real problem. Also, walking fast becomes a real challenge. Jupiterians use special %^*#@—pronounced Ō Ō Ká Ā and translated "Juprite" canes to help them avert obstacles and stabilize their sense of balance.

Finally, a Jupiterian's muscles become weaker over the years because of all the fat and salt in the diet. Special daily exercises on the tread mill and exercise bike are needed to strengthen their muscles. My wife now spends three hours a week at the gym. The exercises seem to be helping her to strengthen her muscles.

Staying away from fat, salt and sugar is a must. Raytonia now exists on a rather monotonous choice of foods. Vegetables, fruit, bran cereal, fish and chicken (only the white meat) make up the bulk of her daily meals. The use of salt is carefully monitored because it along with the fat causes Jupiterian blood pressure to rise.

She is taking about seven pills a day that are prescribed by a doctor on Jupiter. She consults with him about her condition every three months via interplanetary communication. Her supply of medicine has been sent by small satellites from Jupiter. The service has been great. We arrange her pills in a plastic pill carrier every week. Recently, the doctor has added an anti-depressant called a Mint Jupiter. Raytonia claims that it really blows the blues alway—and puts her into outer space.

According to my beloved Raytonia, the hardest thing about the whole business is the loss of spontaneity in her life. Jupiterians are basically fun loving and spontaneous persons in their daily life. So all the regimented injections, pills and exercises along with the monotonous diet make for a loss of joy.

One of the few pleasures in Raytonia's life has been listening to books on tape from the State Library for the Blind and from the Jupiterian Outerspace Lending Library. While she likes mysteries written by Earthlings, she really enjoys the funny novels from Jupiter. They are always uplifting and filled with comedy—so reflective of the harmonious, light-hearted Jupiterian society. It always does my heart good to hear Raytonia laugh and giggle as she hears one of those tapes.

Recently, Raytonia was helped by visitors from Jupiter. Yes, the Jupiterians are starting to visit Earth again with improved saucers. They feel badly that some of the earlier travelers to Earth have had so many problems. Anyway, my wife was given a tune up in one of the "hospital saucers." They sort of rewired her and put in some new parts to patch up her inners. So, she is feeling a lot better. This doesn't mean that she is eating fat, sugar and salt again. No indeed. But the repairs along with the diet and exercise have helped her to feel better.

Now, you may wonder why I stayed married to Louise once I found out that she was really a woman by the name of Raytonia from another planet. Well, to tell you the truth Jupiterians have wonderful minds (she does great on Jeopardy), organizational skills and sweet natures. Raytonia told me that war hasn't existed on Jupiter for 5,000 years. Everyone there is so good at achieving a meeting of the minds that conflicts no longer exist. So, for these reasons it has never occured to me to leave her—or to turn her over to the authorities.

My beloved Raytonia has told me that she could return to Jupiter if she wanted to. The Jupiterians have developed a powerful beam that can transport anyone back to Jupiter within minutes. However, my beloved has refused to leave me. She said, "My life there would not be a happy one after sharing so many wonderful years with my dear Earthling (that's me)."

By the way there are thousands of Jupiterians on Earth—scattered throughout the planet. The Jupiterian philosophers who govern Jupiter became so concerned about Earthlings' love of warfare that they thought some of their agents might be able to keep the peace. And, they certainly have tried. Without them Raytonia claims we would have blown ourselves up long ago—become one of those black holes out in the universe. She claims that many of the winners of the Noble Peace Prize are—you guessed it—Jupiterians. Some of Earth's greatest philosophers, musicians, scientists, artists, government leaders and even actors, comics and fashion designers are Jupiterians.

Well, I feel better now. I needed to tell someone. Please believe me when I say that "the Jupiterians have landed." And, now that you know, you may wish to look a bit closer at the friends in your life—especially if they are smart and have sweet dispositions—they may be Jupiterians. If that proves to be the case, don't go around shouting, "Heavens to Jupiter!" Just accept him/ her as a special gift from the galaxy and—enjoy!

INTERVIEW

What is your name?

Diana Knickers

What makes you smile?

A baby who is smiling.

Do you have a limerick to give us?

I sure do. Here goes.

There is a gal named

Knickers

who loves to lick her

fingers

after she has soaked them

in a bowel of cake batter

that has the flavor of the

candy bar called

Snickers.

The Year of the Ark

My wife and I are serving as Worthy Matron and Worthy Patron of an Eastern Star Chapter. Our grand officer selected as her symbols Noah's ark, the dove, the rainbow and two fun animals—Ginny the Giraffe and Emily the elephant.

We meet with our co-officers in other chapters once a month at the big Masonic temple located in the central west end near St. Louis University. We also have parties in our respective chapters honoring various officers. It gives everyone a chance to know each other better and to plan some fun times.

One of the things that we did was to compose some new lyrics to the tune of "The Notra Dame Victory March" to honor our two grand officers. Here's how it goes:

> Cheer, cheer, for Ri-Ta and Rauel,
> With these two lead-ers we'll nev-er fail.
> The migh-ty Ark will keep us dry.
> Nev-er a wor-ry from the sky.
> We'll go to parties, we'll have some fun.
> While in our chap-ters
> Work will be done.
> In the west we'll serve this year.
> A-sso-ciates both far and near.

After we sing the song, I lead everyone in the Ark cheer that goes like this:

> Bud: "Give me an A!"
> Members: "A!"
> Bud: "Give me an R!"
> Members: "R!"
> Bud: "Give me a K!"
> Members: "K!"

As I give the letters, I form them with my body much to the amazement of all. At the conclusion, we all yell: "Ark! Ark! Ark!" If you want me to give you a demonstration of the "living letters," I'll be happy to oblige.

After doing this at several parties, I was given the nickname of "Arky" which I dearly love.

We have gone all out in terms of ark decorations for regular meetings and special party nights. Most of us have found or made large arks to display in the East—that's where we sit when we preside. My wife and I found large cut-outs of Noah's ark, some doves and a rainbow at a religious store to put up on the wall behind our chairs. I made some arks out of brown construction paper and poster board for table decorations. I filled them with white, blue, red and yellow flowers selected by our worthy grand matron. Many of us have used the Bounty towel with the ark on it for placemats. All of us have used stuffed animals—unusually displayed in pairs—as part of our decorations.

Party games have included the following: pin-the-tail on the elephant, a quiz about Noah and the ark, and ark bingo. Some chapters have put on skits featuring Noah. One is based on a skit recorded years ago by Bill Cosby that is hilarious. In the routine Cosby playing Noah compains to God that he isn't up to building such a large ship. Of course, Jehovah threatens him with hell and damnation. Once the vessel is built Noah faces all kinds of reactions and questions from his neighbors who wonder why he has such a large object in his driveway. Another skit is based on a song about why we don't see unicorns anymore. Of course, the answer is that there wasn't enough room for two of them on the ark.

My wife has been giving and receiving all sorts of gifts featuring the ark. Many are ark music boxes. One plays the tune of "Talk To The Animals." Others are ark wind chimes, ark butter dishes, ark night-lights and ark cookie jars. She was given a cute tea set composed of an ark teapot and cups in the form of various animals—pigs, sheep, elephants. Of course, elephants and giraffes are being given too as gifts since they are our fun emblems.

Under "Good of the Order" I've been gavelling up the members to join me in imitating animals found on the ark—especially the elephant,

Buddy Webb

kangaroo, gopher, alligator and penquin. I'll be happy to illustrate what I do if you are interested. Also I've been telling harmless animals jokes such as:

Two monkeys discussing evolution: "You mean to tell me that I'm my keeper's brother?"

Male elephant as female passes: "Wow! A perfect 258-297-314!"

Fish to swordfish: "The transatlantic cable? Oh you didn't!"

Another fun thing that I've been doing is calling up the chapter and then asking the members to join me in pretending that we are on board the ark and performing such chores as the feeding the animals, mopping up the decks, steering the ship, putting animals back in their cages, mucking out the ship and looking out for the return of the dove.

Recently, one of the members of my chapter who has gotten "ark madness," gave me hand puppets of Noah, Mrs. Noah and several animals. I have used them to welcome special guests as they are escorted to the East. All are delighted to have Noah and Mrs. Noah along with some of their animal friends bid them welcome and to engage in some small chit-chat. People seem to love to go along with the imaginery situation. I think that it brings out the "happy child" in all of us.

I'll admit that we have had a few—a very few—members get a bit uptight by some of the humorous things that we have been doing. But, we simply ignore the "wet-blankets" and do our fun stuff. One thing for sure, people aren't going to sleep during the meetings, and they certainly are smiling and laughing more. And, good fellowship is what the meetings are supposed to be about.

INTERVIEW

What is your name?

    Jim Dig

What makes you laugh?

    Well, when someone tickles me.

Do you have a limerick to share?

    Yes man. Here it is.

        There is this guy named

        Dig

        who really enjoys playing

        gigs

        at all the "dives" and "joints"

        in the dens of

        SIN

Star Days

Last week at our Eastern Star meeting, my wife and I, as Worthy Matron and Worthy Patron, planned an all officers party. It is a time set aside each year for the Worthy Matron and Worthy Patron to honor and thank their eighteen officers—and especially the Associate Worthy Matron and Associate Worthy Patron who serve in the West.

Since next year's emblem is the school house, we decided to carry out a school theme. We purchased black construction paper to make placemats. We used white crayons to make the mats look like chalkboards. Here is what was placed on each mat:

In the center of each of the round dining tables we placed a circular paper post with this sign printed on it: "School Zone—25 mph." We selected yellow napkins to remind people of caution signs and school buses. We also placed in front of each placemat an exercise (a math problem, an exercise involving finishing a logical series, a task of connecting dots to form a picture) that a child might do in school.

As favors we placed at each placemat a brown paper bag labeled, "lunch bag." Inside the bag was a red apple made of red construction paper, a milk carton made out of white construction paper, some pieces of bubble gum and kiddy candy, a small hostess cake and a large square piece of paper that read, 'This is a pretend sandwich. You can get a real one at the lunch counter."

We put up "School Crossing" signs over the entrances to the dining room. On the curtain above the buffet table we had a huge sign which read, "School Cafeteria." The "kids" had plenty of good things to eat. The buffet featured ham and Swiss cheese sandwiches, home-made chicken salad, chips, a wide variety of colorful salads and cold drinks and coffee. For desert, they could have either a chocolate or strawberry sundae.

Under "Good of the Order" all our officers along with many side-liners who had protemed offices and helped at our recent BBQ were escorted by the two conductresses behind the alter. At that point the Worthy Matron introduced each one of them to the audience and thanked them for their dedicated work for the Chapter. Then, as the audience clapped, they were escorted to the East and gifts were distributed. They had their choice of yard signs. One featured a large yellow butterfly with the caption, "Home Sweet Home"- another featured a red lady bug and "Welcome Friends"—another featured a yellow bumblebee and "Buzz On In"—and still another—a pink angel with the caption, "Bless Our Home."

The program took place after the closing of the chapter which involves closing the Bible and removing the paraphernalia. My wife and I had written new words to the song, "School Days, School Days." She rang a school bell as I distributed copies of the song. After that, the organist played through the melody once and then everyone began singing the new words:

> School Days, School Days,
> "Learning about Eastern Star" Days,
> Balloting, business and secret work;
> the Deputy never will let us shirk.
> Proficiency tests, committee reports,
> Bills to be paid—we have all sorts.
> And all is put down in the Minute Book,
> When we go to our Eastern Star.

School Days, School Days,
"Learning about Eastern Star" Days,
We introduce our distinguished guests,
Tell of our sickness and our distress,
Communications left and right,
Square all those corners—do it right!
And all is put down in the Minute Book,
When we go to our Eastern Star.

After that we divided the audience into groups. Everyone was told to share with the group something funny or embarrassing or memorable about their school experience. Then, each group was told to vote on the best story. That person was given a prize (a small bird house with a humming bird) after telling her/his story to everyone in the chapter room.

Here are the prize winning stories:

"When I was in second grade, I had to pee so badly. I remember that I was sitting in a circle with other children hearing our teacher, Miss Warner, read us a story. I was too afraid to interrupt her to ask if I could go to the bathroom. I suddenly couldn't hold it any longer and began peeing. My accident wasn't discovered until after we started putting our chairs back into rows. Then, one of the boys pointed to the large puddle on the floor."

"When I was attending a rural grade school, I went outside with other kids to get a drink at the water fountain. Our teacher, Mr. Leech, had alloted a certain amount of time for us all to get a drink. Well, I was the last to get one. While I was just about finished, the teacher started paddling my butt because the time was up. Needless to say, I was always afraid after that to use that water fountain."

"When I was attending a Catholic grade school, I shared a desk with a boy by the name of Billy Rogers. He seemed to really to like me a lot. One day he whispered that he loved me—and then he kissed me! Well, the nun had a fit. She took both of us out in the hall and beat our hands with a ruler. She also told us that what we had done was sinful—and that we should tell our priest about it when we went for our next confessional."

"I remember going out to the play ground after lunch and jumping rope with other children. They were using two ropes to play Double Dutch. I was jumping away and then the wind blew my skirt up. Well, at that point one of the other girls yelled, 'Hey, look! Patty isn't wearing any underpants. You can see her bear ass.' I had forgotten to put my patties on. I was so embarrassed."

"At my school we had a swimming pool. Well, one day I dove into the water and suddenly found myself being sucked down the sewer. The pool was being drained. I was rescued by my teacher using a bamboo pole for me to hold onto."

"I remember waking up in the morning and feeling very cold. Then, I looked out the window and saw all the new snow that had fallen. I told myself, 'I hope the school bus won't come today. Surely they have called off school.' After breakfast, I started walking up the hill to Gravois to catch the bus. The snow was still coming down. Well, no bus came. I was so happy as I walked down the hill to my house. Well, I'd just gotten into the house, when my mother who had been washing dishes and looking out the kitchen window shouted to me, 'I just saw the bus go by. You better start walking to school young lady.'

The next morning my wife and I received many calls from members who wanted to tell us how much they had enjoyed the evening. We thanked them for their positive feed back and told them that we had wanted to really surprise them and do something special for them because they had done so much for the Chapter and had given us a lot of TLC. They repeated, 'Well, it was certainly quite a special evening—something to remember.' Of course, my wife and I feel the same. But, what we will remember even longer are all the acts of kindness that we have received from so many caring Eastern Star sisters and brothers.

INTERVIEW

What is your name?

Jane Whiggins

What makes you giggle?

Someone who looks cross-eyed at me.

Do you have a limerick to give us.

Baby, I sure do. Here it is.

There is a gal named

Whiggins

Who can giggle

like the diggins

when you tickle

her under her chin

and poke her in her

hind-endie.

The Share-A-Joke Club

We all know that humor is a great tonic in dealing with daily ups and downs. That was brought home to me recently when Louise and I listened to a tape on the importance of humor from the Society for the Blind.

Steve Allen was featured on the tape. He told several amusing stories and then told us that doctors have proven that humor causes a chemical change in the body which promotes health and wellbeing.

Well, after hearing that I decided to form a share-a-joke club among my friends who agree that we sure need a laugh or two to make us forget our troubles and feel better. Since the start of the war in Iraq, membeship in the club has increased greatly.

The club is very informally organized. No roll is kept. No minutes are kept. All we ask is that members call one another when they get a joke that they would like to share. At the present time we have about ten members. In this piece I will simply refer to them by their first names.

Since so many of us spend a lot of time with the doctors, we find that we especially enjoy jokes involving the medical community.

Nelda told a joke featuring an older lady who had gone for her annual check up. Her doctor had told her, "Be sure to bring in all of your medicines so we can review them." Well, as they went from one bottle to another, the doctor was surprised to find a container of birth control pills. He looked at her and asked, "What do you need these for? You're over seventy. You don't need them." The woman replied, "Oh doctor they make me sleep so soundly. I don't have a care in the world." After hearing that the doctor exclaimed, "Hey, I'm sorry but I don't understand." In response the lady explained, "Well doctor, I have a wild teenage granddaughter. Every morning I put one of the birth control pills in her orange juice. Believe me doctor, it sure helps me sleep better at night."

Bill told me this joke about a 92 year old man who had gone to his doctor because he was concerned about his love life slowing down, the doctor asked, "When did you notice this problem?" The 92 year old responded, "Two times last night and once this morning."

Betty told me this one. Seems that this man went to see his psychiatrist because he was suffering from depression. The psychiatrist told the man, "Do what I do to get out of depression. I always call up my wife and make a date for dinner and dancing." Later when the patient saw one of his friends, his friend asked him if he had taken the doctor's advice. The man replied, "Sure did. I'm picking up the psychiatrist's wife at 7:30 p.m. for dinner and dancing."

Ruth shared this joke with me. A woman by the name of Rose wondered if her deceased husband Fred had gone to heaven. She decided to go to a spiritualist to see if she could reach her husband during a a seance. After calling out "Fred, Fred, Fred," she heard, "Rose, is that you? What do you want?" Rose asked, "How are things where you are?" Fred responded, "Oh, it's so beautiful. The sky is so blue—the grass so green." Relieved to find that he was in heaven, Rose asked, "Fred, what do you do all day?" Fred replied, "I eat and make love." Rose exclaimed, "Oh Fred, I'm so happy that you made it to heaven. I was worried." Then Rose heard Fred say, "Heaven? I'm not in heaven. I'm a buffalo living on a prairie in South Dakota!"

Richard told me this one. It seems that this farmer and his mother-in-law were out in the corral one day. As he led his mule out of the gate, it resisted and started kicking wildly. In the process the mule kicked the farmer's mother-in-law to death. Well, the funeral was held several days later. The minister who was going to preach the funeral was amazed by all the men who were in attendance. He looked at the farmer and said, "My, your mother-in-law sure had a lot of friends." The farmer replied, "Reverend, they aren't here for her. They are here to make bids on the mule."

A club member by the name of Meg loves to collect dumb blonde jokes. Here is the latest one that she told me. It seems that this blonde went into an appliance store. As she pointed, she told the clerk, "I want to buy that TV." The clerk replied, "I don't sell to blondes." Confused, the woman left the store and dyed her hair red and returned to the store. Again, she demanded, "I want to buy that TV!" The clerk again said, "I don't sell to blondes." The woman left the store and changed her appearance again. This time she put on a brunette wig and glasses before she returned to the store. Again pointing, she demanded, "I want to buy that TV!" Again, the clerk responded by saying, "I don't sell to blondes." The woman replied, "How do you know I'm a blonde?" The clerk replied, "That isn't a TV. It is a microwave!"

Now after hearing these jokes, don't you feel better. I sure do. I can't wait for the phone to ring to get a new joke.

INTERVIEW

What is your name?

    Joe Spankey

What makes you laugh?

    A clever repartee on a comedy show.

Do you have a limerick to share.

    Hey man, I'm ready.

        A man named

            Spankey

      had a pet

          monkey

     by the name of

         Mickey.

     He would do tricks

        as long as he got

    bananas instead of

       spankies.

My Life Has Gone To The Dogs

I truly love dogs. Of course, some people, like my wife, would say it is a fetish because of the way dogs have taken over my life. There was a time when my wife issued the following ultimatum: "It is either me or the dog. You either get rid of that dog or I'm walking out that door." I was able to stop her by assuring her that "our" dog really loved us both equality. Peggy (the dog in question), thank God, read my mind and gave my wife a few wags and a juicy lick (a big kiss to a dog lover) on her face.

My parents purchased my first dog when I was about five years old. They hoped that I would learn a lot of responsibility by taking care of a pet. They choose a female cocker spaniel that had beautiful reddish brown hair (I refuse to use the word "fur"—sounds like a wild animal) and large black eyes. I named her Patsy. I remember my father telling me, "Buddy, be sure Patsy has plenty of water at all times. Feed her on time. Take her out for potty and a good walk at least two times a day. And, be sure to brush and comb her every other day."

Patsy became my constant companion. Naturally, she slept at that foot of my bed. She was first "person" (for that is the way I look at a dog) who I saw in the morning and the last one I saw at night. Patsy loved to go with me to play with other children in the neighborhood. I remember that during the winter she loved sledding. I would place her between my legs and then we would go down the steep hill near 12th Avenue.

After my wife and I were married we got a male Pekingese who we named Ming. He had beautiful long white hair over most of his body except around his eyes and ears. Those areas were covered with lovely reddish brown hair. Ming wasn't too smart—never did learn many tricks or words. His favorite game was running after tennis balls. Because of his long hair, he required a lot of grooming. But, I didn't mind because he could be so sweet. Once when my wife was in the hospital for a long stay, Ming felt neglected. I remember coming home and sitting on the davenport to read the newspaper. Then, all of a sudden I found Ming coming through the newspaper that I was holding. I got his message loud and clear. I gave him a big hug, lots of petting and some reassuring words.

Our next dog was a fox terrier. She was white with a black spot around her right eye and a large black spot on her left side. She was so cute as a puppy. I recall that my wife put her in our rural mailbox so that I could take a picture of her peering out of it. Peggy was very smart. She learned how to sit up, roll-over and play dead. She also had quite a vocabulary—"popcorn, ice cube, peanut butter." Because we got her in July, she developed a fear of popping sounds because of all the fireworks. Also, she disliked storms and would always go under the bed when a storm approached. She loved to ride in cars. Every time you opened the car door, Peggy would jump in and sit on the back seat. Then, she would refuse to get out. Often, I would say, "O.K. Peggy, I'll give you a ride." So, I would drive around the block and go back into the garage. Only after that would Peggy get out. Another favorite game that she enjoyed was barking under the bed as we tried to change the sheets. She loved playing the wicked troll.

After Peggy died we purchased three Chihuahuas—a tan one named Cindy, a black one named Cleo and a white one named Crystal. They were all very sweet but rather dumb compared to Peggy. Cleo was one of the most domineering dogs we ever had—she had to be supervising everybody. Also, she was very selfish. For example, she would take chew toys away from Cindy and Crystal and hide them. Poor Cindy became a nervous wreck because of Cleo's bullying. Crystal was the smallest and the smartest. She also had the best disposition—very calm and comforting. Only Cleo and Crystal slept in our bed. Cleo insisted that Cindy stay out of the bedroom. Finally, I got a regular dog bed for Cindy so she could at least sleep under the night table. All the dogs liked to go into pillow cases and under small blankets. You had to watch where you sat because you never knew when you would sit on a sleeping Chihuahua. We still have Crystal. She enjoys being the only dog. Her favorite game is to protend that the vacuum cleaner is a dangerous alien. As soon as the "alien" appears she starts barking and attacking it. She has a ball.

As part of my devotion to dogs I have collected a lot of stuffed toy dogs. When Taco Bell came out with small stuffed and talking Chihuahuas, we had to have them. There is one with a rose in its mouth. It says as you push its tummy, "I think I'm in love." There is another one with a bib around its neck. It says, "I'm getting hungry—very hungry."

Also, I have quite a collection of statues of dogs. Several are five inches tall. The best ones have large expressive eyes that say, "Take care of me." The exception is a poodle with a very mean and crazy look. I still like it because it is so unusual. I have a statue of a crocker spaniel with huge soulful eyes. It is so sweet that you want to take it up in your arms. Then there is a brown dachshund with a tear coming down from one of its eyes. I have one statue that looks like Cleo as a puppy—black with a white bib and white paws. I have a lot of miniature statues too. One is a fox terrier who is resting on his front paws with his rear end up in the air.

Since my friends know I love dogs, they send me cards featuring cute dogs. Also, several people have given me doggie magnets for my refrigerator.

Naturally, I love to read stories and books about dogs. My favorite author is James Herriot, the British vet, who had such a deep understanding of the close relationship that can develop between a dog and a person. Since I'm a great fan of the Roosevelts and especially FDR's dog Fala, I can read over and over again when FDR got Fala, how he trained him to do tricks, how he protected Fala from fans cutting off snips of his hair, how he defended him against charges that he had cost the taxpayers a lot of money and Fala's reaction to FDR's death— running through the back screen door of the Little White House at Warm Springs, Georgia. I also love to read about how Fala would continually look for his dead master. Whenever he would hear sirens, he would raise his head expectantly—hoping to see a car bringing his beloved master back to Hyde Park.

While I have been involved with many groups, I think that the one that I have contributed the most to is the Humane Society. I especially send money to the Society when I hear and read news accounts of cruelty to animals and terrible conditions in so-called "puppy mills."

Whenever I see puppies in a pet store window, my inner child emerges and I start singing silently to myself, "How much is that doggie in the window? The one with the waggelly tail? I do hope that that doggie's for sale!" Why? Because dogs have been a great comfort in my life. Dogs have given me a lot of unconditional love and devotion—two commodities that are in short supply in this life, especially among our own species.

INTERVIEW

What is your name?

    Red Potato

What makes you laugh?

    That's easy. A surprising punch line to a joke.

Do you have a limerick to share with us?

    Yes. Here goes.

        There is a guy named

            Potato

        who loves red

            Tomatos.

        Not only the ones

            that grow on vines

        but dance on stage.

        He especially loves the

            tomato

        who is the top

            banano.

The Unsung Star of "The Wizard of Oz"

As I was going through the new arrivals at the Tesson Ferry branch of the County Library, I came across the autobiography of one of the unsung stars of the movie "The Wizard of Oz." It was recently found by Willard Carroll during the expansion of the Ventura Freeway from a site that was once a pet cemetery. The scrapbook was kept by Terry the terrier who played Toto in the film. It was enclosed in a nine-inch metal box.

Terry who played Dorothy's faithful, somewhat scruffy-looking dog is in virtually every scene of the film. In fact, Terry is actually in more scenes than Judy Garland, though she doesn't have as many close-ups. However, there are nine shots in which Terry has the screen completely to herself. On top of that, Terry has 44 barks in the movie.

One of the most important emotional aspects of the film is Dorothy's special unconditional love for her little dog Toto. And vice-versa. We all remember how we shared Dorothy's distress as Miss Gutch prepares to put Toto in her basket and take her off. We all sense Dorothy's emotional need to keep Toto close to her as she finds herself in the strange world of Oz. We all reacted with fright as Toto is threatened by the wicked witch and her helpers—the Winkie Guards and Winged Monkeys.

Terry's autobiography was filled with all sorts of memorabilia—photographs of herself with other stars like Spencer Tracy and Shirley Temple, ads about some of the films she appeared in, reviews of her performances by the critics, her contract with Metro-Goldwyn-Mayer Pictures, parts of the script for the Oz movie, and her official MGM studio portrait that was sent out to her fans upon request.

She says that she was born in Alta Dena, California in 1933. She thinks that she had some brothers and sisters but can't be sure. She does remember her mother nursing her however. When she was still a puppy she was taken by a family that she really did not get to know very well. They seemed to shout a lot and became upset because she failed to peepee on newspapers that had been put down in the kitchen. She found herself being very upset by the whole experience. The next thing she remembered was being put in a car and driven a long distance until it drove up to large building set far off from the road. She found out later that she had been enrolled in the Hollywood Dog Training School operated by a recent immigrant from Germany by the name of Carl Spitz. Carl had trained dogs in Germany for the blind. He had come to the United States to help discipline and train dogs for dog lovers and also for those who wanted their dogs to appeared in movies.

According to Terry, Carl took a real liking to her. She found herself enjoying making him happy by following his hand signals to do all sorts of tricks or "routines" as Carl called them—sitting up, rolling over and playing dead. He was so pleased with her that he allowed her to spend a lot of time with his family in their home. Eventually, Carl adopted Terry when her real owner suddenly disappeared without paying the bill for her training.

Then, one day in 1934 Carl took Terry for a long drive to the Fox Studio where she was introduced to a beautiful, smiling little girl with lots of curls. Terry remembered liking her a lot. The two of them ran around and played a lot together. Then, the little girl—who turned out to be Shirley Temple—declared, "She is hired."

Well, Terry found herself appearing in her first movie which was entitled "Bright Eyes" with Shirley. Terry played the part of Rags and she had almost as many lines as Shirley did. Besides barking, Terry as Rags did a lot of other routines—running, jumping, sitting up, rolling over and looking at the camera with a tug-the-heart look.

Terry received great reviews when the film came out. Suddenly she became a hot property and offers started pouring in. The next big part was in "Fury" with Spencer Tacy. According to Terry, "Spence" as she called him was a dream to work with. She learned a lot from him—about how to underact to achieve the best effect. Spence had that down pat. Terry said that you never really thought that he was acting at all—just acting natural.

After that film she was hired by the great Cecil B. DeMille to appear in "The Buccaneer." It was Terry's first costume picture. She hoped for a lovely costume like everyone else was getting but she had to settle for a flea bath, a nail trim and—an enema. While she made a lot of money working on the picture, she preferred working with Spence.

Then, came the opportunity to play Toto in the Oz film. She got the part because she looked like the little dog illustrated in the book. Terry had to learn a lot of new routines because the script called for a lot of things that she had never done.

According to Terry the more she read the script the more she realized that the whole story wasn't about the Oz—but about her. She wrote: "I have the closest relationship of anyone to Dorothy. I'm why she runs away from home. And, why she does all sort of things to save me from something called the wicked witch."

Terry liked working with all the stars in the film and especially Judy Garland who was very friendly and helpful. The only actress who scared her was Margaret Hamilton. Terry had met her before she was made up and really liked her. Then, a weid woman with a green face appeared— with a pointed hat and long fingernails. She started yelling at Terry and trying to grab her. Well, poor Terry became so frightened that she did #2 right there. She was so embarrassed. But, everyone on the set just laughed and seemed to understand. Margaret even apologized for coming on in such a vicious way. Meanwhile, the "mess" was cleaned up by the stage crew.

In her autobiography Terry tells the reader about the two most difficult things that happened to her while making the movie. One was working with the so-called "Winkies"—the creatures who helped the wicked witch. One of them stepped on poor Terry's paw. She found herself so terrified and in pain that all she could do was cry and think to herself, "I wanna go home!" The other one involved running away from the "Winkies" and the Winged Monkeys in the wicked witches' castle. At one pont she had to jump on a draw bridge which she had never done before in any other picture. But, she gave it her all and everything worked out fine.

The most enjoyable thing that Terry did in the film was to sit on a harvesting machine and listen while Judy sang "Over the Rainbow." Terry remembers that at one point she had to raise her paw—on cue— and give a tug of your heart look which she had by that time mastered.

There was a wrap-up party after the film was finished. All the stars signed Terry's scrapbook and wrote a lot of nice things in it about her too. Judy was especially sad to say "goodbye" to Terry. Judy even had tears in her eyes when she handed Terry over to Carl for the last time.

Terry and Carl went to the premier of the film. The reviews were really good—especially for Terry's performance as Toto. There was even talk about putting Terry's paw prints in cement at the courtyard of the Grauman's Chinese Theatre. But, then the subject was dropped and never brought up again.

Terry who was now renamed "Toto" appeared in many other films. During World War II she helped sell war bonds by making a tour of the United States along with a lot of other famous dogs.

According to Willard Carroll, Terry died in 1945 and was buried in the backyard of Carol Spitz's Hollywood Dog training School.

Willard Carroll feels that one of the reasons why people like to see **The Wizard of Oz** again and again is because they love to feel the special relationship between Dorothy and her little feisty and loveable dog Toto as they share some terrifying experiences in the Land of Oz.

After reading the book I appreciate the acting job that Terry gave to the part of Toto. When I see the film again, I'm going to look at Toto in a different way—I'll remember the story of Terry and also observe more closely the fine performance that she gives in the film. I hope that you will do the same.

INTERVIEW

What is your name?

    Bonnie Shampoo

What gives you a giggle?

    Oh, I think a funny rhyme.—silly rhyming slang.

Do you have a limerick to share?

    Sure do. Here it is.

        There is a gal

            named Bonnie

      who goes to the pool

          wearing only

          a blue bikini.

      Her figure attracts

          all the studs

      who think that she is

          very sexy and

          quite a sweetie.

We loved to see Terry in all of his films. He made us smile.
Identify the dogs as—Duffy and Fluffy

Dealing With My Hat Fetish

I love to wear hats, look at them on others and feel their brims and the materials and decorations that they are made out of.

For a long time now I have recognized that my love of hats isn't normal. It is one of my many fetishes. Often, I find myself trying to control the desire to "pinch" someone's hat because I find it irresistible.

Several weeks ago, Jake appeared in one of her most beautiful hats—the off-white one with the wide brim. The crown is decorated with a black sash with white polkadots. I looked at it with great longing. I wanted to seize it right there and run out of the door with it. Of course, my reason prevailed and I found myself saying, "Oh Jake, what a super hat!" But, while I was saying it, I was also thinking, "Perhaps I can 'pinch' it when she isn't looking." I even thought of different places to stash it in the room—one of the cabinets—the waste basket—the ice-cream freezer. Of course, I thought that I would have to distract everyone's attention while I took the hat and hid it. I thought, "I could yell, 'Look! There is a rat!'" And, once Jake discovered that it was missing I would turn to her with my most astonished expression and ask, "Jake, are you sure you wore a hat today? I can't image anyone wanting to steal it."

I have tried very hard to understand how this hat fetish came about. In my quest I have discovered that my wearing hats goes way back. I have found black and white photos of myself as a child. In some of them I'm wearing little knit caps—in others sailor hats, cowboy hats, baseball hats and party hats. In several I'm dressed up in a suit to go to Sunday school and on top of my head—yes, you guessed it—is a minature man's fedora hat.

Perhaps the fetish came from my parents and other relatives. I remember my mother had all sorts of hats in her closet. I can see her now sitting at her vanity and looking in the round mirror as she tries on different hats. They were all sorts of shapes and colors with all kinds of decorations on them. I was especially drawn to decorations—feathers, imitation jewels, pearls and doves. I will admit that I tried several on; I especially liked her berets. I recall too that she loved getting compliments on her hats. It made her feel good about herself—it confirmed her good taste and sense of style.

My dad and my Uncle Chester liked hats too. Dad was bald and used hats to cover it up. He liked fedora hats. I can't remember that he wore them at an angle. Now, Uncle Chester did. He was a sharp dresser with his tailored suits and wide variety of hats. He like fedora hats along with homburgs. I remember that he was a tall, lean guy with a rugged but handsome face and an outgoing personality. He told me why he wore his hats at an angle. "Buddy," he declared, "the ladies like men who have a rakish look." By the way, he may have been right because the ladies were very much attracted to him. Even at sixty-five he was still going strong sexually. His third wife who was twenty years his junior told my mother on the q.t. that Chester liked sex at least twice a week. Perhaps my interest in hats is connected with the image that Uncle Chester gave me of what makes for a virile man—a hat. Could be.

Another influence probably came from movies. Most of my silver screen heroes wore hats—Roy Rogers, William Powell, John Wayne and Fred Astaire. I especially remember that Fred liked to wear his hats at an angle when he danced.

I distinctly remember that the men in my neighborhood who were given the most respect wore hats. I recall that Mr. Good would arrive in his purple Packard usually wearing a tweed homburg to inspect the truck farm that supplied vegetables and flowers to his estate. Everyone would be so solicitous as he was given an up-date.

Mr. Wood who had his own large home in the neighborhood was another man who always wore hats. I can see him now driving by in his black '39 4-door Buick or simply walking around the neighborhood. He would tip his fedora as he smiled and said "Hello" to his neighbors. He was always greeted with respect and admiration.

I have tried to understand my hat fetish by approaching it from Freud's theories about fetishes. He claimed that a sexual connection with whatever—rubber, feathers, fur, leather, shoes, etc—had caused the fetish. One connected the sexual good feeling and release with the object that was closest at hand. Could it be that I had some of my first sexual encounters wearing a hat? I really can't remember anything like that. But, perhaps, I have suppressed it. Who knows? Of course, perhaps the other party was wearing a hat during our pleasurable moments together. I'll have to think about that more.

Over the years I have had many hats that I have truly loved. I tend to bond with a few hats and try to make repairs on them so that they last forever. One hat that I really liked—but alas is no more—was a magnificant homburg that was made of corduroy and was a beautiful shade of forest green. I always wore it with the brim down and at a rakish angle. I wore it with a forest green corduroy suit and a forest green corduroy overcoat to match. I usually always carried a black unbrella with the outfit. I really looked terrific. It was part of my so-called English period when I wanted to be mistaken for a young scholar from England.

Another hat that I have worn for years—at least eighteen years—is a homburg made of a grey tweed material. Again, I always wear it with the brim down and at an angle. I have had to repair it again and again. The last time I purchased a new feather for it and added an ornament. I remember that I always wore it on field trips along with my London Fog overcoat. The students loved the look. They enjoyed teasing me about looking like the bumbling private eye named Columbo who used to be on TV years ago.

I have a blue—gray tweed hat that I like a great deal. It is also fairly old. I have repaired it on several occasions. It goes with a lot of blue and grey outfits that I have.

During the really cold winter days I often wear a fur hat that is decorated with a red feather and a silver ornament. It looks great with my heavy winter coat that has a fur collar.

As a teacher I often wore hats that went with costumes that I used to make certain lessons more interesting. One was a black pilgrim's hat—pointed with a gold buckle—that I wore with a long black cape. I wore it when I lectured about Puritanism. Uusally around Halloween I would wear it as a gag. As I started crumbling to the floor, I would shout, "I'm melting! I'm melting!" The students loved it.

When I presented lessons that required the students to solve problems, I dressed as Sherlock Homes and wore a Deerstalker hat. It was always a good way to introduce a problem involving examining evidence that had been given to the students. I always had my large round magnifying glass in my hand as I challenged them to carefully examine the documents, pictures and other objects that they had been given.

Finally, sometimes when I presented material about Germany I would appear dressed in lederhosen with knee high socks and on top of my head would be a beautiful green Barvarian hat that had a high crown and featured a bright red feather and a silver ornament.

Now, dear listener, if you have any hats at home that you don't know what to do with, please remember me. I will be happy to take them off your hands. I promise that I will clean, repair and treasure them.

Also, watch out, my fetish may cause me to "pinch" your hats. The other day I was strongly drawn to Jake's red beret. I even thought that I heard it saying, "Bud, come and get me." I was able to control the urge—but you never know when it will overwhelm me. That's the nature of fetishes you know.

"Oh! Watch out!—I just saw a big rat scamper across the floor."

INTERVIEW

What is your name?

    Ben Bedpost

What gives you a chuckle?

    Well, its when a doggie stands up and then spins around.

Do you have a limerick to share.

    Of course I do. Here it is.

        There is a man named

           Bedpost

        who loves to hang from

         lampposts.

       He takes off his

         pants

       and moons people

        as he howls

      to the moon.

Troublemakers

I decided to write this piece as a result of being very disappointed with certain people who are members of an organization that I belong to. I will not mention the organization because the obligation that I took on joining it prohibits me from making negative remarks about it. However, to relieve my frustrations I decided that the topic of troublemakers in organizations would make for a great piece for our writing group. Here is my list of ten types of troublemakers that I have found in practically every organization that I have belonged to:

The Malicious Gossips

Despite the fact that most of the organizations that I belong to prohibit members from speaking evil of a brother or sister, there are malicious gossips in them who do so. These admirers of Truman Capote usually get on the phone and spread all kinds of terrible things about other members. I have heard everything from "she takes money from the treasury" to "he is gay" to "watch your husband—she is after anything in pants" to "I swear he pinched my butt—so girl, watch out!"

The Power Fanatics

There are many who are in to CONTROL in many of the groups. They want to CONTROL every aspect—from who will be admitted to the group to who will be elected to offices to how the money will be spent. What really makes the situation bad in some organizations is that you find two groups (I call them Neo-Stalinists) battling each other for CONTROL.

The Machiavellian Enthusiasts

These descendants of Cesare Borgia love to plot and scheme to undermine someone—to pull off a *coup d'etat*. Of course, they find co-conspirators among the malicious gossips and the power fanatics. The Machiavellian enthusiasts get their "kicks" out of plotting and scheming. They should try to "get a life" but they don't seem able to do so. I guess they are having so much fun planning their next power move, that they really don't have the time.

The Closed Minded

These members (Let's call them the Neo-Romanovs) refuse to entertain any new idea with regard to keeping records, reading minutes, handling correspondence, raising money, changing membership requirements, ritual and the by-laws. They certainly have a way of turning off new and younger members.

The Rules of Order Devotees

These sons and daughters of Moses carry a copy of **Robert's Rules of Order** and **The Constitution and By-Laws** of the particular order and expect everyone under all situations to follow and obey the rules to the letter. They delight in catching someone who is violating a rule. While they can be helpful to provide information when asked, they often create a mountain out of a mole hill. In other words they usually create a fuss over something trivial in nature. I guess it's their holier than thou attitude that turns me and others off.

The Misers

These stockholders in Scrooge Incorporated don't wish to spend any of the organization's money on worthy causes—or anything else for that matter. They think that the organization's money is their money. They forget that the organization is supposed to be doing charitable things with the money that is raised and not hoarding it in CD's.

The Title Enthusiasts

These members are in love with their exalted positions and insist that they be introduced with their proper titles and especially receive the proper honors due to their exalted positions. In many of the groups I belong to I find the titles really funny at times. Of course, I keep this to myself. But, judge for yourself. How about these: Supreme Worthy Commander, Supreme High Priestess, Supreme Watchman of Shepards, Supreme Royal Patron, the Most Worthy Grand Matron. Many of these title enthusiasts get very upset if they are not given their moment in the spotlight. In some cases "the exalted one" will publicly reprimand the person who introduced them incorrectly. In my opinion they are on ego trips and are more engrossed in their titles and honors than encouraging brotherhood and charity work by the members of the organization.

The Strict Ritualists

These sons and daughters of John Calvin will correct people who fail to get the ritual letter-perfect. I think it is their attitude that causes trouble. So often when they correct someone they do it in an angry and threatening way. This approach turns other members off so that they refuse to fill any stations.

The Goldbrickers

These members never show up to do any of the work—or if they do they spend their time talking or eating rather than helping out. And, when it comes to the clean up, they are long gone. So, the same people wind up doing the work again and again.

The Big Spenders

These lovers of Marie Antoinette want the officers and membership to spend a lot of money on frivolous things—fancy officer's dresses and tuxedoes, expensive banquets, trips and parties. They forget that the organization is supposed to stress spending money for charitable projects.

Boy do I feel better. Sorry for being so catty but I often find the above intolerable—especially when they ask, "Why aren't our members coming to meetings and participating?" Usually I try to keep my humor, remember all the cooperative and caring members that I have met in these organization, and keep appealing to the good common sense of the majority of the members in dealing with the "unspeakable ones." Thanks for listening. What is your take on this topic? Have you met any of the above in the organizations in which you are a member?

INTERVIEW

What is your name?

>Goldie Bee

What gives you a belly laugh?

>That's easy. It's when I go out with my friends and we line dance at a club. I'll admit that I have a few drinks before I go on the dance floor. Also, the music must be really wild and crazy.

I bet you have a honey of a limerick for us.

>That's right.

>>There is a gal named

>>Bee

>>who buzzes around

>>like a Queen Bee.

>>She hopes to attract a

>>male bee who

>>will help her populate

>>her hive—

>>but not rule it—

>>because she is after all

>>the Queen Bee

Alfred Kinsey Becomes Part of Pop Culture

How would you like to find yourself so famous that you become part of pop culture? I found out vicariously by reading a biography about Alfred Kinsey.

James H. Jones's account of Kinsey's life is very scholarly and well written. One learns so much about the man and the wellsprings of his scientific interests and research. While most of the chapters in the biography are serious in nature, I found a lot of humor in the chapter that relates how the general public reacted to the publication of Kinsey's **Sexual Behavior in the Human Male** in 1948.

Within months following the publication of his detailed sexual study, Kinsey became an icon of popular culture, even celebrated in music. For example, Martha Raye, that lovable, big-mouth singer and zany comedian, produced a jukebox hit when she recorded Phil Moore's "Ooh, Dr. Kinsey." Julie Wilson also put his story to song, delighting audiences with a little ditty called "The Kinsey Report." And Tin Pan Alley churned out a batch of catchy tunes with titles such as "The Kinsey Boogie" and "Thank You, Mr. Kinsey."

Poets, too, took turns lionizing and vilifying Kinsey in verse. An anonymous master of that inherently indecent verse form known as the limerick wrote,

> "There was an old phoney named Kinsey
> Whose ideas of fucking were flimsy
> He knew how to measure
> A penis for pleasure,
> But he came much too quick in a quim, see?"

By the way the slang word "quim" was used in the 18th Century to refer to a VAGINA. Don't feel bad if you did not know. I didn't either. I finally found the word in one of those huge dictionaries at the library.

Playwrights quickly discovered that references to Kinsey got laughs. In Detroit, a producer of an off-color play even went so far as to mention Kinsey in a newspaper advertisement, promising "the bare facts about the subject Dr. Alfred Kinsey discussed in his book." Also radio did not ignore him either. In one episode, Sam Spade, the top-rated dedective, investigated a murder of a chauffeur named "Kinsey Martin Pomeroy." Martin and Pomeroy were two of Kinsey's top research assistants.

Of course, Hollywood got on the bandwagon. Producers tried to purchase the film rights to Kinsey's book. Many thought that they could make a great film out of it and of course also a lot of money. Others had their research staffs study the work in order to determine how they could make their films have more "mass male sex appeal."

As you can imagine, Kinsey's research topic also attracted comments by such sex pots as Mae West. In an open letter to Kinsey published in **Cosmopolitan**, Mae offered to compare notes, one sex expert to another. "Your approach is scientific: observing, investigating, classifying, statistical," she wrote. "Mine involves at least the first two of those methods, but, when it comes to statistics, I'm afraid the only figure I employ is my own. And that figure, which as become internationally familiar, stands for sex—just as your report of facts and figures does." And, she was right. In the popular mind, Kinsey quickly became known as "the Dr. Gallup of Sex" or simply as "Dr. Sex." Booksellers who were asked the book's price often quipped, "Sex-fifty."

Naturally, professional comedians had a field day with Kinsey. Nightclub jokers specialized in "blue" one-liners, while radio comedians settled for tame gags such as "If it's OK with Kinsey, it's okay with me" and "He's at the awkward age—you know, too old for the Bobbsey Twins and too young for the Kinsey report."

Folk humorists, too, explored the comic potential of Kinsey's research. Expressions such as "hotter than the Kinsey report" and "Kinsey-crazy" entered the language.

Meanwhile, on the campus of Indiana University where Kinsey had spent his life teaching, Hoosiers started calling Kinsey's base of operations "The Sex Center." Students on campus circulated a mock petition proposing to change the name of a popular necking spot from the "Passion Pit" to "Kinsey Hall." One of the newspapers on campus published a cartoon showing a solitary girl's snow tracks leading to a women's dormitory late at night, beneath which appeared the caption "Evidently she doesn't read Kinsey."

Everyone seemed to want to cash in on Kinsey's name. Citing Kinsey, a prominent fashion designer, brought out a new line of dresses "designed to influence behavior in the human male." Steamy novels were touted as "fictionalized Kinsey reports." A Newark psychiatrist's survey of teenage morals was advertised as a "bobby-sox Kinsey report." **Clinical Sonnets**, a book of poems by a Boston psychiatrist, was heralded as a "Kinsey report in verse."

Even a liquor company got into the act. When its customers started mailing in labels and bottle tops requesting free copies of Kinsey's book, the Kinsey Distilling Corporation of Philadelphia, distiller of Kinsey Whiskey and Kinsey Gin, took out a newspaper ad explaining that the company had no relationship to the famous sex researcher but wished him well.

Politicians climbed on the bandwagon, too. At the the Republican National Convention in 1948, delegates appeared with campaign buttons bearing the inscription "We want Kinsey, the people's choice." That same year, Kinsey got one vote to Harry S. Truman's twenty-seven and Dwight D. Eisenhower's twenty-six at the annual Cherry Blossom presidential poll in Washington, D.C.

You are probably wondering how Alfred Kinsey responded to all this attention. Well, believe it or not, he took it in stride. He was thrilled by the book's reception. The professional and academic community lauded the book as one of greatest scientific works since Darwin's **On the Origin of Species.** They were happy that an area of human behavior which had been largely hidden by foolish conventions and taboos was now out in the light of day.

While Kinsey was surprised by how he had suddenly become an icon of popular culture, he seemed to be at the same time delighted by the whole experience. He got all sorts of fan mail. For example, Vance Packard wrote to say, "I have followed with fascination your rise to the position of America's Most-Talked About Man. You certainly have inspired some new phrases for the English language. Did you have any idea the book would create such a hullaballo? I overheard one of my students at NYU refer to another student sarcastically by saying, 'Oh, he's Kinsey-crazy.'" Kinsey replied, "I knew, of course, that there was going to be considerable public interest, but I had not realized that it would develop into quite so large a proposition."

After reading about Kinsey's experiences as an icon of popular culture, I'm all set to be discovered too. It should be a lot of fun. Don't you agree. I can't wait to see what limerick will be written about me. I'm sure it will be a humdinger.

INTERVIEW

What is your name?

> Clem Beanbag

What gives you a smile?

> Playing a practical joke on someone.

I bet you have played a lot of jokes on people. Do you have a funny limerick for us?

> Yes on both. Here goes my limerick.
>
> > There is a man
> >
> > > named Beanbag
> >
> > who never had anything
> >
> > > in his bag.
> >
> > Life was up and down
> >
> > > for him.
> >
> > He never could count
> >
> > > on a fix or
> >
> > something being in the
> >
> > > bag.
> >
> > Even his devoted wife
> >
> > > looked like a
> >
> > > hag.

The Bottle And I

Dear reader, I hate to disappoint you but this piece is not about a drinking problem. However, it is about another sort of addiction—my love of and fascination with bottles. My wife claims that it is one of my many fetishes—along with hats, statues of dogs, books about Franklin and Eleanor Roosevelt, and pictures and photographs of nudes—both women and men. Well, enough of those fetishes. Today, I'm going to tell you about my love for and attraction to bottles. Perhaps I can write other pieces about my other "turn-ons" in the future.

I am drawn to bottles for a variety of reasons. I like their different shapes whether they are tall, short, fat or skinny. I love their colors—amber, green, purple, blue, and rose. I love to see the sunlight stream through them and illuminate them. I love the fact that many are in the form of famous people, log cabins, animals, and famous landmarks like the Eiffel Tower or the Tower of Pisa. I love to read the inscriptions that appear on some of them. Some are very funny while others reflect a certain time period.

How or why I have this obsession with bottles is anyone's guess. I really don't know. Perhaps I was drawn to the perfume bottles kept by my mother on her dresser. I remember that she had as many as six such bottles—all shaped differently and each of a different color. Perhaps I associate beautiful bottles with my mother's love for me and her beautiful radiant smile. Or, perhaps it is because my father kept a large liquor cabinet filled will all sorts of bottles with a variety of liquor in them. I remember the tall, gleaming whiskey, wine, scotch and burboun bottles. I recall that some were in the shapes of birds, famous landmarks, ships, and animals. I have often wondered if my father dangled multi-colored bottles over my crib to amuse me. Who knows? Who cares? I only know that I am in love with bottles.

I started collecting bottles as a child and later as a teenager and adult. I remember asking my father for his unusual liquor bottles. The clear ones I would fill with dyed water and then place them on the window sills so that they could catch the light. I remember wanting any liquor bottle that was in the shape of a car, eagle, ship, famous person or landmark. I placed them all around my room. Later, I began to buy bottles that were unusual at regular stores or at sales in the neighborhood. I remember that during the bi-centennial I purchased all sorts of bottles.

While I have enjoyed expanding my collection, my wife hasn't. Every time we have a garage sale, she asks, "Bud, why don't you put some of your bottles in the sale?" Every time we move she asks, "Bud, do you have to keep all those bottles?" I, of course, respond to these questions as if my life has been threatened. I just can't give them up. I still don't think that she understands the depths of my compulsion to obtain, nurture, and love bottles.

I have several bottles that are shaped to resemble the Liberty Bell. Of course, the crack in the famous bell is featured along with the inscription, "Liberty Bell." They are in a variety of colors—green, yellow, blue. They were made in Taiwan by the way. I am sure that the people of that island could have cared less about our bi-centennial and more about the money they would make preying upon our patriotism. Come to think of it perhaps that is why the bell is labelled, "The Liberty Bell." They were made by the Taiwanese. Any American, just by seeing the crack, would have known immediately that the bottle represented the Liberty Bell.

I also have two large bottles—one green—one yellow—in the shape of George Washington's head. The following words are inscribed below George's head: "Continental General of the American Army." At the base are the words, "Simmon's Centennial Bitters—Mt. Vernon, Virginia." The bottle was manufactured in Wheaton, N.J. I am not sure that it is actually modelled after a bottle of the period or not. Also, I am not sure that we can assume that George drank a lot—of the bitters that is.

Another usual bottle that I have is a tall one for medicine. On the front of the bottle is the image of a large safe with wheels on it. The following inscription is featured on the front along with the safe: "Frank's Safe Kidney & Liver Cure." On the back is the following:

"Since 1892 Works Wonders. This is not a polite way of drinking. Nothing in this remedy will grow on anyone. No danger of contracting the drink or any other kind of habit." I gather from the statement that some people who took such medicines became addicted to them—or used them in place of hard liquor.

I have in my collection several bottles in the shape of a log cabin. The most attractive is rose in color and has the following inscribed on the front: "E.C. Booz's Old Cabin Whiskey." This bottle was also made in Wheaton, N.J.

Another interesting bottle is shaped in the form of a horse shoe. It is green in color and features on one side a horse which is running and the inscription, "Horse Shoe Medicine." On the other side is a close-up of a horse's head and the inscription, "Horse Shoe Bitters." While the bottle has Collinsville, Illinois on the front, it was made again in Wheaton, N.J.

Another handsome bottle is green in color and features on one side a glass house in Wheaton, N.J. with the year 1888 above it. On the other side is supposed to be the face of Benjamin Franklin. I say supposedly because Ben looks thin and younger than our usual image of him. Over the image of the man is "Benjamin Franklin." I'm not sure where it was made. But it has all the characteristics of something made by those Taiwanese again.

One of the more unusual bottles in my collection is a tall amber bottle which features the tree of life and the following inscription: "Straubmuller's Elixir—the Tree of Life Since 1880." On the other side it reads: "Nectar of the Golden Life of Health and Vitality." I gather that elixirs were very common in the 19th Century. In my opinion many people demanded these so-called "health stimulants" because they were often high in alcohol.

Another of my favorite bottles is yellow in color and features on one side the face of Liberty surrounded by small stars and on the other side is the American bald eagle. There is no inscription on the bottle—nor any place of manufacture. I figure that it was made in the U.S. since the creator felt that we would know the identities of the figures on the bottle.

I have a lot of whiskey bottles in the shape of ducks, turkeys, pheasants, sailing ships, and famous people. My favorite is a large blue eagle that is about fifteen inches tall. I love these types of bottles for their colors and their often funny or dramatic qualities. For example, the bottle in the shape of Napoleon is quite amusing. He has a stupid expression on his face. By the way you open the bottle by turning his hat.

I have to admit that while I enjoy my bottles, I am a bit troubled by my compulsion to love them—to protect them—to feel responsible for them. I can't seem to part with them; it is if I am being asked to sell my very soul. So typical of a fetish don't you agree. And how does one deal with it—or does one simply continue to collect and enjoy and leave it to others to figure it out. I think that is the way I want to handle it. At the present it makes me feel special—unusual. Being a victim of a fetish makes me into a colorful character. Don't you think so? By the way do you have any old bottles at home that you want to part with? I assure you I will love, honor and obey their every wish till death do us part. So, how about it dear reader?

INTERVIEW

What is your name?

    Jennifer HoHO.

What gives you a giggle?

    Reading a funny limerick.

Do you have one to share?

    You bet!

        There is a gal named

           Ho Ho

    who denies she is only

        interested in being

out for studs so she can

        be a ho.

When tagged with that label,

        she shouts "noo" and

adds she likes a good time

        but she would never

take money for her hohoing.

Rescuing Clarence

As I was walking around my apartment complex, I went by one of the large green dumpsters and found sitting there a large brown lion. Don't be alarmed. It wasn't a real one. It was a stuffed lion. Well, as an animal lover—as a member of the Humane Society—I found myself stopping and looking intently at the lion. It was quite large—four feet high and two feet wide—with a beautiful mane, a large black nose and a long tail with a tassel at the end. The lion had a delightful whimsical grin and large black eyes that were crossed.

I thought to myself, "Perhaps someone has moved into one of the apartments and can't find room for him." I decided to continue my walk thinking as I did, "Surely someone—a child or a parent—will want this delightful stuffed lion. It deserves to find a nice, warm and friendly new home."

After I had gotten back to my apartment, I took off my coat, poured myself a cup of coffee and sat down next to Louise. I told her about the lion. When I mentioned that it was crossed-eyed, she exclaimed, "Bud, that is Clarence the crossed-eyed lion. A few years ago, Disney made a film about the story of Clarence." I told her about how handsome he was and about my hopes that some child would adopt him.

The next morning, I got up as usually, dressed, had a cup of coffee and then left the apartment to get a newspaper from the vending machine near the club house. As I walked toward the vending machine, I looked up the street and saw Clarence still sitting by the dumpster. I found myself becoming concerned about his welfare. I could see that the sky was clouding up. I remembered that the forecast called for heavy showers. After getting a **Post Dispatch** I decided to walk up to Clarence to see how he was doing. Once I got to him, I looked at him and then was astonished to hear him say, "Oh, sir, please take me home. I won't be any trouble. I don't eat or drink anything—and I can bring a lot of fun into your life." Well, the next thing that I remember was carefully reaching down, picking Clarence up and gently putting him under my arm. As we walked toward the apartment, I told Clarence, "Now, now Clarence, everything is going to be fine."

Once I got Clarence home, I had to quickly find a suitable place for him in the living room before Louise woke up. I hoped that she would let me keep him. After considering various places, I put him next to the book case. Then, I got the rug cleaner and gave Clarence a nice shower. I also combed out his beautiful mane and tail so that he would make a good impression.

I waited patiently for Louise to wake up and come into the living room. I wondered how long it would take for her to see him—she has been having trouble seeing things from a distance. Well, much to my delight when Louise came into the room, she spotted Clarence right away and exclaimed, "Oh Bud, it is Clarence. Isn't he adorable. I can see why you liked him."

Louise suggested that we dress him for each holiday. She declared, "Clarence will be our fun conversation piece." She immediately suggested putting one of our Santa Claus hats on him and around his neck a big red bow. Well, Clarence seemed so pleased. Indeed, I think he smiled even wider when I took his picture in his new Christmas outfit.

The only member of our family who seemed at first to have some reservations about Clarence living with us was Crystal our little white Chihuahua. She went over to Clarence and gave him the once over— she smelled his large paws, mane and rearend. She especially seemed fascinated by the fluff at the end of his tail. In fact, she began chewing on it. I finally had to tuck Clarence's tail under his butt so that it would be safe. Gradually, Crystal went about her business and did not bother Clarence which was a relief both to Louise and myself because we did not want to have to choose between keeping Crystal or Clarence. What a terrible dilemma that would have been!

Clarence has been with us now for about two months. He gives us such comfort and joy. He has a way of looking at things that is so positive—so cheerful. Many an evening he has entertained us with funny stories of his adventures going from one household to another. And, he has so many hilarious stories to tell. The best ones involve an exotic dancer named Miss Fanny who was his owner for about a year.

Not only did he have the privilege of seeing the Divine Miss Fanny perform on stage, he also saw her in action back at her apartment. Clarence—with a sly grin and laugh—usually ended his tales by declaring, "It was quite an education—even for a lion who has seen just about everything." He has also become popular with our visitors. They all find him to be so entertaining and down right refreshing. As one friend recently declared, "Where in this world can you find someone so gifted at telling an amusing story like Clarence?"

The other day I was telling Louise that I was certainly surprised that some child had not rescued Clarence before I came along. Louise looked at me and smiled and said, "A child did rescue him dear—his name was Buddy."

INTERVIEW

What is your name?

    Ted Squirrel.

What makes you laugh?

    Seeing clowns do tricks.

Do you have a limerick to share with us?

    I'm ready if you are.

Well, go ahead.

        There is a guy named

          Squirrel

      who is well named because

        he runs as fast

      as a sports car on a highway

        and he likes to wave

    his "tail" to invite gals

        to share his nuts

  with him in his leafy

      hideaway.

ThoREau's HEaVEnly Disobedience

Time: the present
Place: Purgatory
Scene: a conversation between the angel Gabriel and Henry David Thoreau

The angel Gabriel approaches a construction site and asks the supervisor to tell Henry David Thoreau who is busy working on the roof of a small cabin-like house to come down and talk with him.

A well-built man of average height with an untrimmed beard and a pensive look out of his large gray eyes comes toward Gabriel and asks, "So Gabriel, what do you want? I hope you won't keep me long because I need to get back to work. More poor souls are expected to arrive tomorrow and they will need housing."

"Henry, what I have to say won't take long. His Blessedness, the Almighty, feels that you have spent enough time in Purgatory."

"Well Gabriel, I'm really surprised. His Blessedness knows how I feel about Him and the universe He has created. He knows that I feel that He has played a big joke on humankind. And, this human doesn't think it is funny. So, Gabriel I can't understand why He has changed His mind about me and wants to transfer me out of Purgatory."

"Well Henry, the Almighty feels that your positive contributions to humanity more than make up for your insubordination and skepticism."

"Contributions? What do you mean?"

"I'm referring to **Walden** and your essay entitled, *Civil Disobedience*. Both works have had a great impact."

"Are you sure? Not many copies of my book sold in my lifetime. And that essay got me in a lot of trouble with those supporting the war with Mexico."

"Well, what you don't know is that parts of your works were printed in textbooks throughout the world. Also, millions of students are required to read both your book and essay."

"You don't say. Well, I'll be damned!"

"And, that isn't all. The site of your cabin near Walden has been marked by a metal plaque. And the site of the jail where you spent a night because you refused to pay your taxes is considered a revered landmark. Besides that, a bronze statue of you along with a replica of the cabin you built stands near one of the entrances to Walden Pond."

"What! I can't believe it. The last time I heard about Walden was from a lady who told me that the pond had been polluted. She told me that people loved to throw empty Pepsi-Cola bottles into it."

"Well, that was true. However, in recent years the authorities have cleaned up the pond and passed laws making littering a crime."

"I hope so. It was such a beautiful and quiet place. As you know, I wrote some of my best work in that little cabin in the woods by the pond."

"Yes, yes, I know. By the way do you know where your cabin furniture is now?"

"No, where?"

"On display in a museum in Concord. Thousands of tourists go through the museum every year. They especially pause in front of the table upon which you wrote your famous works. After that, they usually head over to the site of the cabin at Walden Pond."

"O.K., O.K. Gabriel, so I'm famous. What I would like to know is if people are following my ideas—loving nature, resisting being enslaved by machines and taking action against what is morally wrong. From what you say about people polluting Walden, the whole planet has probably gone to hell. Even in my day those dirty, noisy and smelly locomotives were polluting the air and poisoning the beautiful country side. I bet people have become slaves to machines too. I can recall the terrible conditions in those New England textile factories—they were hellholes for the poor devils who had to work in them. And how many people are taking action against wrong doing? Hell, even in my day most humans were a bunch of sheep. Baa, baa, baa!"

"Now Henry, calm down. If it will make you feel better, I can assure you that environmental groups are trying to protect nature. And while machines have increased in type and number, there are many in the arts and humanities who are constantly reminding people that they must not lose their humanity—that they must take time to look within themselves as well as reconnect with their neighbors. By the way, your essay on civil disobedience has been used by a lot of people to stand up against acts of tyranny. Don't you remember meeting Mohandas Gandhi and Martin Luther King, Jr.? They are both in Purgatory."

"Well yes, I met them but His Blessedness has kept me so busy building houses for the new arrivals that I never had the chance to discuss anything with them."

"Well, both of those men used your idea of civil disobedience to free their countrymen from oppression."

"You don't say. So, why aren't they in Heaven?"

"Well, His Blessedness, the Almighty, has a few reservations about them. King loved the ladies, if you know what I mean, and Gandhi's peaceful demonstrations often turned violent."

"That sounds like His Blessedness. You know Gabriel, He sure can be petty at times—and oh so self-righteous. I think that He fails to look at the big picture. Well, I'll tell you, if King and Gandhi are going to be forced to stay in Purgatory, I'm staying here too."

"You're what?"

"I'm staying right here!"

"Please Henry, the Almighty wants you in Heaven."

"Doing what?"

"Well, He thought you would enjoy either working in the Heavenly Forest or teaching about the wonders of nature to the children. What do you say?"

"I say, tell the Almighty to take His offer and shove it up his blessed ass!"

"Why Henry, I can't tell that to His Blessedness. It might cause Him to send you to Hell. You don't want that to happen do you?"

"No I don't. But, there are times when I really get fed up with Him. Like I said before, I'm still mad that he put humans in the universe without any explanation as to where they came from or why they were sent to Earth. They weren't given a clue. They were just left to fend for themselves. And then to top it off, if the poor devils didn't figure it out—get the right answers, they were sent off to Purgatory or even worse Hell."

"Oh Henry, please calm down. I'll tell you what, I'll go back to the Almighty and tell Him that you would like King and Gandhi to be transferred to Heaven with you."

"O.K. Gabriel, my boy, you do that. I'll go if he accepts both of those good men. By the way, take my advice and catch His Blessedness on one of His good days—when He is the Almighty of the New Testament and not the Old. Good luck!"

After Gabriel leaves, Henry goes back to work and thinks to himself, "I haven't felt so good since I spent the night in the Concord jail. Perhaps this time my civil disobedience just might work."

INTERVIEW

What is your name?

    Betty Darling

What makes you giggle?

    Seeing Miss Piggy in a puppet show.

Do you have a limerick to share.

    I sure do. Here it is.

        There is a beautiful

            gal named Darling

        who isn't only pretty but

            sweet and caring.

        Dating her is like going

            with a glamorous nurse

        who meets your physical needs

            and has time to be

        sensitive to your emotional

            entanglings.

Flash Mobs

The other day as I watched The Early Morning Show a feature appeared about a supposedly unusual phenomenon called "flash mobs." I use the word "supposedly" because to me it is simply a part of or a variation of "street theatre" that has been around for a long time.

In the case of "flash mobs," a group of people (about 20 to 35) suddenly and unexpectedly appear in a public place and engage in some type of activity. In some cases words or slogans will be spoken as the people engage in their physical exercises. Usually the so-called "mob" is trying to make a point about some social issue or aspect of daily life.

When I was team teaching in a course called Humanities at Webster Groves High School back in the '70s, the drama teacher, Mrs. Ernestine Smizer, taught us all (both teachers and students) about street theatre and then supervised actual "street happenings." This came only after giving us the fundamentals of drama and doing improvisations.

One of the aspects of street theatre is that nobody should know about what is going to happen until the event. According to Ernestine that was the only way it would be effective and truely a pure form of the concept of street theatre. This, of course, eventually got her into trouble with the our principal, Mr. Jerry Knight.

The first spontaneous happening occurred in the two rest rooms on the first floor which were located near the front entrance. During the break between classes, students found that the signs on the doors of the restrooms had been changed. Both were marked with signs saying "Co-Ed Restroom." They also saw numerous boys and girls (students or "actors" from our Humanities class) going into and out of the restrooms. Well, you can imagine the reaction. It put people in a state of shock. While some simply stood with their mouths open, others were pointing and yelling, "Look what they are doing!" By the way Ernestine thought that event was one of the most successful dramatic happenings that she had ever directed. Indeed, she gave all the students who participated in the happening "As".

While Ernestine was delighted with what had happened, Jerry wasn't. He immediately called the Humanities team to the office and demanded to know what we were up to. Ernestine wasn't a bit intimidated by Jerry's request. In fact, I remember Ernestine telling the rest of us before the meeting, "Now don't worry. The man just needs to be educated about street theatre. Once he understands, he will go along with it." Well, it didn't entirely work out that way.

During the meeting Ernestine explained to Jerry that she was only using street theatre as a teaching method to help students become more confident about using various techniques of drama. She also explained to him that street theatre was often used to bring attention to public issues. In fact, she said the students in he recent dramatic happening were only highlighting how ridiculous it is to have so much separation of the sexes in daily activities.

I have to give Jerry credit for at least hearing out Ernestine's explanation. However, after she finished, he remained largely unconvinced. While he allowed us continue to use street theatre as a teaching method, he insisted that we keep him informed about when and where we intended to supervise the next dramatic happening. Of course, we had no choice but to accept his demands.

Of course, Ernestine wasn't too happy about Jerry's restrictions. I can still hear her declare, "Well, what can one expect from a former math teacher."

The next event took place in the cafeteria during the lunch hour. It was centered on what had happened in one of the restrooms on the second floor. A restroom had recently been painted by a group of students who were interested in improving the school. They had decided that it would be nice besides repainting the walls to paint a mural on one of them. They settled on a lovely pastoral scene.

Unfortunately, shortly after the job had been completed, several students vandalized the painting. As a result, the administration ordered the janitors to paint over the entire mural. Naturally, the students who had painted it were very upset because they were willing to paint another.

The dramatic event, which of course this time Jerry knew about, involved a funeral service for the wall with the mural. It took place in the cafeteria and then the court yard.

While students and teachers were in the mist of eating lunch, a long line of Humanities students appeared bearing a black casket. They paraded the casket through out the cafeteria and then went to the court yard for the burial.

A student by the name of Mike Wallace had written an eulogy for the event. It was so unusual and well done that I kept it among my teaching souvenirs. I should mention that Mike was dressed like a priest as he read it. Here it is:

"Dearly beloved we are gathered together in this lovely setting in the presence of God and these witnesses to pay a last tribute to the late and beloved Mr. John Wall of restroom 201.

"Those of you who knew him, know that he was a strong and beautiful wall. He was created by the loving and artistic hands of Webster Groves students. The artistic designs which filled him, won him many friends and much admiration. He will be greatly missed.

"In the prime of his life he was cut down by evil hands. John did nothing to warrant such brutal treatment. He was here only to give joy and pleasure. Instead, he was cut down in the bloom of his youth by insensitive neurotics. While we feel sorry for the persons who committed this senseless act, we can't forgive their motives.

"Our hearts go out to John's widow - the East Wall - and his lovely children - the North and South Walls of restroom 201.

"It is our sincere hope that John has not died in vain. Let his death symbolize the need for mankind to care for beautiful things and to respect the rights of others to enjoy beauty.

"We commit his spirit to the Great Wall in the Sky. May John find peace and everlasting life in the spirit of the Great Wall.

"We now commit his remains to the Earth, from which he came. Ashes to ashes, dust to dust, and wall to wall. Amen!" Then other members of the funeral party sharted shouting, "Amen! Amen! Amen!"

The reaction to the funeral was one of surprise and awe. I can still remember seeing expressions of disapproval on the faces of many staff members who were trying to eat lunch. I'm sure some were thinking, "What is that crazy Ernestine up to now?" However, the students generally seemed fascinated with the event. Many accompanied the funeral party outside to the court yard and joined in with the "Amens."

Other dramatic happenings occurred throughout the year. The students certainly gained confidence in expressing themselves through drama. They also learned that street theatre can be a powerful tool to educated the public about social issues.

Needless to say, I'm all for "flash mobs" and look forward to more accounts of their occurences. I only wish that the media people would educate themselves about street theatre and its long history in making a positive contribution to human society.

INTERVIEW

What is your name?

    Jacob Fancypants.

What gives you a belly laugh?

    A comic doing a comic bit in drag.

Let's hear a limerick from you.

    Sure. Here goes.

        There is a guy named

            Fancypants

      who can really

          dance.

Put him on a dance

        floor and he

becomes the prince of the

        light fantastic.

While he doesn't look

        like Kelly or Astaire,

put him on a dance floor

      and he is transformed

from fancypants to fancydance.

How To Knock Someone Off

Haven't we all wanted to knock someone off? What? You say that you would never do such a thing—that you feel highly insulted that I would imply that you are capable of murder. Oh, come on now, be honest. Haven't we all met someone—known someone who became so detestable that we secretly thought about his/her demise (we never called it murder)—and then much later actually thought of ways to do him/her in? By that time we had reached the point where we felt that we were totally justified in taking (what we called) "a positive step" to remove the detestable one from the face of the earth. We would say to our ourselves things like: "It would be best for everyone." or "She/he serves no useful purpose but to make others miserable." or "He /she even hates himself/ herself—It would be a blessing if he/she is taken out of his/her misery. We would be doing him/her a favor." Indeed, we might by this time think about recruiting others who also hate the "unspeakable one" (never the victim) in order to mastermind a group or co-op murder like the murder of the foul and disgusting Rachett in **Murder on the Orient Express.**

Now, if you are looking for ways to knock off your intended victim, I believe that no other source is better than the writings of the famous Agatha Christie. As you know, she wrote all sorts of novels, plays and short stories about murder. In order to keep her reading public coming back for more, she found all sorts of ways for the murderers to bump off their intended targets.

Dear Agatha often created murderers who used poisons—cyanide, strychnine and good old reliable arsenic. Also, the old girl often had her killer use snake venom. One female victim was killed on board an airplane by a dart dipped into venom. It was sent flying through the air and into the lady's neck by a blow gun. Some say poison is the favorite method of killing used by women. That sounds sexist to me. I'm sure Lizzie Borden would disagree too. The only problem with using poison is that today the police have at their disposal sophisticated lab techniques to ascertain the cause of death. Also, one would have to buy or get the poison somewhere and that might be difficult to do without leaving a trail. So, while poison is an option, it should be used after careful thought.

A safer method might be to administer in some way an overdose of a medication that the victim takes on a regular basis. Agatha often had the killer see to it that the victim took an overdose of insulin or a heart medication like digitalis. The death then would be seen as a case of suicide or an accident by the authorities.

Those of you who have read dear Agatha's works know that she found murder weapons everywhere. She was quite ingenious—indeed in some books she showed herself to be a great one for improvising—when it came to the instruments of death. While she included a lot of murders by guns of various types, she seemed to prefer cruder methods which made for more blood and gore—more shock to the reader who was forced to visualize the victim being killed: the horrible surprise on the part of the victim—his/her agony in dying—the mess that it left at the scene.

Agatha liked her sharp instruments. Often people were killed by stilettos, kitchen skewers, surgical knives and razors. They made for some grisly murder scenes. The only problem with anything that involves too much blood is the cleanup problem. You—the killer—or should I say "the agent of God's wrath"—would have to clean yourself up and that might be difficult. Wearing a raincoat—or should I (Ho! Ho!) say "blood coat"—to the site of the killing would be a give away to the intended victim—or at least raise some serious questions in his/her mind. Therefore, it is not recommended. Of course, some believe that Lizzy Borden killed her parents in the nude which made possible a fast cleanup thereafter. However, let me be clear, killing someone in the nude is also not recommended. It could only be done under the most ideal conditions. Think what would happen if someone would come along unexpectedly—or if your victim awakened or turned around. No, that type of thing is pressing your luck too far—especially if you have some distinctive mark on your body such as a birthmark on your butt.

Often, dear Agatha would have the victims strangled. The murderers often used things on the spot to do the jobs—nylon stockings, scarfs, silk belts and raincoat belts. In one mystery the murderer used an ukelele string! Boy, you can't get more clever than that. It makes one want to avoid anyone who plays a stringed instrument. Right?

Some of the poor devils were done in with sportings goods. Yes, in one story the murderer used a golf club to give the hated one a good bashing. In another dear Agatha had the perpetrator use a tennis racket. The racket had been modified—a left hand knob from an old fashioned fireplace fender had been screwed onto the upper frame of the racquet. It made for a very deadly blunt instrument. Indeed, one could say that the victim died of a backhand to the skull. Not very sporting in my opinion. But, they say at the Agatha Christie Fan Club, "All is fair in love and murder."

Dear Agatha often used things around the house as weapons for her many killers. How clever! A paperweight slipped into a woolen sock made for a mighty powerful instrument of death. Of course, the good old standby—the fireplace poker—was often used. No big deal about that. But, in one mystery the killer picked up the sandbag tube that was being used to prevent drafts from coming in under the front door and used it to kill his victim. Talk about improvising! In several stories Agatha had the killers grab heavy statues to use as bashing clubs. In one, the statue of Venus is used in such a way. Of course, some of the killers had a wide range of statues to choose from and naturally selected the one that could do the job and also serve as a symbol of their reason for murdering the victim. Of course, one must remember that someone like Hercule Poirot or Miss Marple may be assigned to the case and he/ she may be clever enough to connect the symbolism of the statue with one of the suspects—that's you—in the case. Oh, yes, in one story, dear Agatha had the victim electrocuted. A chess set was connected to a "hot" chessboard by a wire leading to an electric device in the apartment below. What a shocking way to go! But, that's Agatha for you.

Sometimes Agatha had the killing take place outside. The killer used something in the environment as a weapon. In one mystery the victim is pushed in front of a train. In another she has the killer push the hated one over a cliff. In still another a woman is killed by a cuern—a primitive grain mill—that was hurled at her head. She had looked out her window and had gotten the surprise of her life. And finally, one killer used a heavy granite boulder to killer his victim. It came rolling down a hill toward the surprised victim and crushed her to death. The only problem of using something out in the open is that someone may spot you. Thus, it should be undertaken carefully.

In conclusion, I hope that I have provided some ways that might be useful in your "noble undertaking. "What? You all say that you do not need any of this information because none of you would ever commit murder.

Everyone starts singing: "An evil curse on your head Buddy Webb, Buddy Webb. May you fall and break your head Buddy Webb, Buddy Webb. May God Almighty kick you in the ass Buddy Webb, Buddy Webb."

Bud: "O.K.! O.K.! Enough already! I apologize!" (while he thinks to himself, "I better apologize or I may be a victim of a co-op murder.")

INTERVIEW

What is your name?

Ruby Petunia

What gives you a smile?

When I see someone kiss a baby, a pet or their boyfriend or girlfriend. I get a warm feeling and tingle all over and smile.

Gosh that is wonderful. Do you have a limerick to share?

Yes. Here it is.

There is a girl

named Petunia

who looks a bit peculia.

She likes a

kinky look to attract

fellows who like

to pollinate flowers and

gals named Lillie

and Petunia.

Mugged at The Baseball Game

Every time the St. Louis Cardinals play the Chicago Cubs, you know it is going to be a battle. The three games that the two teams played in Chicago over the July 4 weekend were no exception. My Cubs managed to win the middle game of the series, but the Cardinals won the other two. The first game, played on July 4 itself, was a real heart breaker for my team, because the Cardinals scored 11 runs.

After the weekend's games I felt that I had been mugged, and that gave me an idea. Certain people who work in and around St. Anthony's Hospital love to tease me about being such a rabid Cub fan, and they love to rub it in when the Cardinals win.

On Monday, the day after the series, I had an appointment with my cardiologist for a routine blood test. The last time I had seen Dr. Gafford, he had produced a baseball bat and proceeded to explain to me that it was a "corked" bat. He was referring to the recent incident in which Sammy Sosa, my favorite Cub player, had mistakenly taken to the plate a bat which turned out to contain a piece of cork. Sammy used the bat in batting practice before the game to entertain those fans who like to see him hit long balls.

I decided to play a little joke on the good doctor. I put some red food coloring on a 3" x 3" bandage and placed it on my left cheek. I put Band-Aids on my chin, nose and the right side of my forehead. I also put one on the logo on my Cubs cap. Bud got out his water colors and painted a couple of beautiful "black eyes." To complete the effect, I put a sling on my left arm and decided to use a cane that we keep in the car.

Before I visited the good doctor's office, I decided to stop by the Cardiac Rehab Center which is in the same building. This was where I had spent over a year exercising after my heart attack. The employees there learned early on that I was St. Louis' #1 Cub fan. They teased me mercilessly throughout the baseball season that year. I often dropped in after completing the program just to remind them that the Cubs were still playing baseball.

When I limped in, I was greeted by clucks of sympathy and looks of concern. Everyone asked, "What happed to you?"

I had my story ready.

"Well," I began, "I was on the north side of Chicago last weekend, and was walking along minding my own business. All of a sudden I was attacked by a group of men."

My listeners stood with their mouths open, urging me to go on with my story.

"I could see that they were wearing light gray suits with some kind of red bird on the front. They were caught, and I found out their names."

I pointed to my left arm in the sling and said, "Mr. Pujols did this!"

Pointing to the large bandage on my left cheek, I exclaimed, "Mr. Edmonds did this!"

Then I pointed to my other bandages and blackened eyes and mentioned the names Renteria, Perez, Rolen, Williams and Matheny.

I pointed to the Band-Aid on my cap and said, "Even Tony LaRussa got into the act. This is where he hit me!"

As I spun my Pinocchio-like tale, grins began to spread accross the faces of my listeners. One of them, Nancy, said, "I figured you were up to something when you mentioned the gray suits with the red birds." We all had a good laugh. Of course, one wiseacre had to ask, "Were you hit by a corked bat?"

Then it was off to Dr. Gafford's office. The receptionist looked at me pathetically and asked, "Oh, my dear, what on earth has happened to you?" I told her my sad tale and she began to laugh as the tale went on.

When the nurse called me in, I told her about Dr. Gafford's baseball bat and that I was returning the favor. She went to get him, and he came out carrying the bat. He laughed at my story and said he wanted to take my picture. I struck a very pathetic pose. He said that he would make me a copy of the picture.

When he asked me if I had ever been to Wrigley Field, I replied that I only saw the Cubs from my living room. He told me that every

Muslim must go to Mecca at least once in his life time and every Cub fan should make at least one trip to Wrigley Field.

I guess it is a sad commentary when one feels her life is so dull that in order to enliven it she has to dress up like a mugged baseball fan. On the other hand, it could be that I miss that part of teaching when I would dress up in a costume or plan some other outlandish attention-getter to present a lesson. Could be.

INTERVIEW

What is your name?

> Mel Foxy

Well Mel, what gives you a giggle?

> Reading the comics—especially anything dealing with the relationship of a husband and wife.

Do you have a limerick to share.

> Sure do. Here it is.

> > There is a man

> > > named Foxy

> > who could be

> > > very cocky

> > when doing business

> > > or managing a

> > game of hockey.

> > But, he learned to tame

> > > his ways when a

> > lady beat him at chess

> > with a move called

> > > "tackle and lasso"

> > the King's lackeys.

A Petition To Help Miss Emily

Time: the present
Place: The kitchen at Purgatory Towers
Scene: a conversation between the angel Gabriel and Miss Emily Dickinson

The angel Gabriel enters the kitchen and asks to speak to a cook by the name of Emily Dickinson who has just put a pan of brownies into the oven to bake.

A petite, shy lady with red hair and dressed in a long white dress with a blue apron approaches Gabriel and asks in a small breathless voice, "Did you wish to see me Mr. Gabriel?"

"Yes I do. I'm here to tell you Miss Emily that His Blessedness, the Almighty, is considering moving you from Purgatory to Heaven."

"But Mr. Gabriel I'm perfectly happy where I am. I love making cookies, brownies and cakes. As you know in life I always gave the children goodies and made presents of fruitcakes to my many friends at Christmas. Also, I still enjoy writing poems at the kitchen table while I wait for my pastries to cook in the oven."

"Yes, I know all that. And we appreciate your work here in the kitchen all these many years. However, His Blessedness, the Almighty, feels that perhaps he was wrong in sending you here in the first place and that it might be time for you to leave Purgatory."

"But, dear Mr. Gabriel I was always such a skeptic in life. I'm surprised by this development. After all, I mistakenly—as I found out later—doubted the existence of His Blessedness, the Almighty. Besides that, when I got to the Gatekeeper of the Heavenly Towers and asked to see the Oversoul, I was immediately denounced as—and I quote—'one of those crazy New England Transcendentalists' and sent packing to where I am now."

"I know—I know—but recently a large number of learned souls who in life taught American Literature have arrived in Heaven. After settling in, they asked to meet you. And, of course, they are all surprised to learn that you're in Purgatory. So, yesterday, they petitioned His Blessedness, the Almighty, to reconsider your placement. They told Him that your poetry has done so much good down on Earth and that you deserve to be in Heaven despite your few shortcomings."

"Gabriel, I'm totally confused. I only had a few poems published during my life time. As I recall, they were not read by a lot of people."

"Yes, I know. But what you don't know is that your sister Lavinia after your death had most of your poems published and they were well received."

"Oh my! How could she! Mr. Gabriel, I have always been such a private person. How could she violate my privacy by publishing my innermost thoughts?"

"Oh Miss Emily, let me assure you that your sister had the best of motives. She felt that your insights into the human condition should be read by others. And, according to the professors, she was right! Your poetry has had a positive impact on mankind."

"Are you sure? Not many people buy books of poetry."

"Well, in your case your poetry was also published in textbooks that were used in English classes throughout the entire nation. Indeed, many of your works are required reading for students in high school and college."

"You don't say! I can't believe it."

"And, that isn't all. The house that you shared with your family in Amherst has become a shrine."

"Oh, come now, dear Mr. Gabriel, I can't believe that."

"Yes indeed. Thousands of tourists every year tour your home. The curators even have your white dresses on display. And in your bedroom, they display the basket that you used to fill with goodies for the children. Remember how you would lower it on a rope to the children waiting below?"

"Yes I do. But—but, I find all this too overwhelming. Have I become an icon?"

"Well, yes in a way you have. The locals even refer to you as 'the Mystic of Amherst.' In fact, a few years ago a metal silhouette of you was placed in a park down the street from your home. You are there talking with another poet who you don't know by the name of Robert Frost."

"The Mystic of Amherst! Oh my! It sounds like I have been made into a saint—Saint Emily! Don't you and His Blessedness, the Almighty, find that to be sacrilegious?"

"No, no! Not at all. Miss Emily, you never sought such a position. According to your supporters in Heaven, it is your beautiful and thoughtful poetry that has caused people to pay you tribute. According to them, your poetry is a breath of fresh air in a world consumed with materialism, violence and war."

"So, Mr. Gabriel, things haven't changed much."

"That's right. In fact, during the 20th Century things got worse if you can believe it."

"My, my, you don't say."

"Yes indeed, according to the learned professors, if it wasn't for poets like you, humanity would have really gone to the dogs. By the way, thousands visit your grave every year. Do you know the inscription on your tombstone?"

"I haven't the faintest idea."

"It is this: 'Called Back.' Do you remember using the phrase?"

"Yes I do. It was the last thing that I wrote in a letter. How nice to have it on my tombstone. By the way, this other poet—Robert Frost— what has become of him. Is he in Heaven?"

"No, he is in Hell. Unlike you he had quite an ego problem so he has been sent to the Woods of Hell to cut and stack fire wood all day. He seems to be improving. Nothing like cutting wood all day to make you humble."

"Oh, the poor fellow! Perhaps someday he will be transferred to Purgatory. Most of the people who write poetry are a harmless lot."

"Perhaps it will happen someday. As you say, most poets are basically harmless. In my experience most are quiet, inward-looking souls. Meantime Miss Emily, His Blessedness, the Almighty, has another concern. As a result of the learned professors petitioning for your transfer, His Blessedness secured copies of all of your poems and He really can't understand any of them. They seem to Him very obscure.

But, if you can help Him understand a few of them, He may transfer you to Heaven. Would you be willing to do that?"

"I'll try. Of course, I wrote a lot of poems and so I may not recall the circumstances under which they were written."

"O.K. Here is one that really mystified His Blessedness:

> 'I stepped from Plank to Plank
> A slow and cautious way
> The Stars about my Head I felt
> About my Feet the Sea—
>
> I knew not but the next
> Would be my final inch—
> This gave me that precarious Gait
> Some call Experience—'

So, what are you saying here?"

"Well, I can see why he would have problems with that one. Like so many of my poems, it is a type of first-person retrospection. In it I'm expressing the idea that our minds shield our disasters and abysses from us so that we can successfully negotiate them, stepping around, across, and eventually on."

"I'll tell that to His Blessedness. He has difficulty understanding how your poetry can really be understood by ordinary people. He also wonders if the themes you address are universal enough to help humanity."

"So, let me understand the implications of what you are saying. His Blessedness, the Almighty, may transfer me to Heaven. What will I do there?"

"His Blessedness is willing to let you either work in the Heavenly Gardens or recite and discuss poetry at weekly heavenly poetry gatherings. You will be meeting with some very good and famous people. For example, John Milton has been a regular at the poetry readings for years. So, what would you prefer?"

"I'm a bit shy of crowds so I don't think I would really enjoy the weekly poetry gatherings. And, I know for sure that I would feel very uncomfortable meeting Milton weekly. He always seemed so sour to me—and his poetry so Old Testament-like. But, I have always loved gardening and would love to get my hands in the soil again and work with flowering plants. So, tell His Blessedness, the Almighty, that I want to help out at the Heavenly Garden."

"Will do! Now, you will have to wait at least a week for His decision."

"Dear Mr. Gabriel, I confess, I'm still mystified by how little me could have made such an impact. But, if His Blessedness decides that I have made a positive contribution and wants me in Heaven, I will be happy to go there."

A week later.

"I'm sorry Miss Emily but His Blessedness has rejected the petition to transfer you. He finds it impossible to understand your poems. They are all too introspective. He wonders how the professors ever explained them to their students. Indeed, He is considering transferring the professors to Purgatory. He has also come to the conclusion that your popularity is a result of an overzealous Amherst Chamber of Commerce trying to promote tourism."

"Well, I'm not surprised. Frankly, I'm happy that I get to stay here in Purgatory. I've met so many colorful people here. All free-thinkers of course. I'm sure I would have missed them all. Ben Franklin has been such a delightful companion at meal time. And, Thomas Jefferson has kept me so well informed about a whole range of topics. And then there are those newcomers—Katherine Hepburn and Bob Hope. Kate is so outspoken and Bob is hilarious. And, of course, there is the kitchen. I sure have enjoyed making goodies for all the residents here.

"By the way Gabriel, before you go, would you like to try my brownies? I have a batch cooking right now. They will be out of the oven in five minutes. My brownies are delicious if I do say so myself. In fact, I'm going to bag-up an even dozen for His Blessedness. After all that time trying to understand my poetry, He needs something to sweeten him up. Who knows, He may eventually transfer me not because I can write poems—but because I can bake some darn good brownies."

INTERVIEW

What is your name?

> Mayble Geek.

What gives you a smile?

> Oh that is easy. When I see someone opening a surprise gift. Their reaction to the gift always makes me smile.

Do you have a limerick to share?

> Yes. Here it is.

> There is a girl
>> named Geek
>
> who is very proper
>> and pure.
>
> She will never let a
>> guy take a peek
>
> under her dress or
>> down her blouse.
>
> She is very uppity
>> but not very
>
> smart when he comes to men.
>> But, she may learn
>
> that a peek may result in
>> a peck on her cheek.

Coffee Talk

Time: Now

Setting: The TV Show **Coffee Talk**

Characters:

Linda Richman—hostess (sincere, nervous, uses hands a lot)

Sarah Bernhardt—(proud, coquettish, confident)

Franklin D. Roosevelt—(confident, gossipy, funny)

Lucille Ball—(friendly, funny, confident)

Mahatma Gandhi—(quiet, introspective, devout)

Adolf Hitler—(cranky, punitive, confrontational)

Dialogue

Linda: "Welcome! Welcome to Coffee Talk where famous guests chat about their likes and dislikes. I'm your host Linda Richman. Oh darlings! I'm so excited. Look! (she holds out her quivering hands) I'm tingling all over. Let me take a deep breath and start. (she breathes deeply) Today, we have some very famous people on the show. On my left we have Sarah Bernhardt the world famous actress."

Sarah: "*Bon jure mes amis.* I am the Divine Sarah!"

Linda: "Next to the Divine One is President Franklin D. Roosevelt."

FDR: "Hello, my friends out in TV land. It is grand to be here!

Linda: "Next to President Roosevelt is Mahatma Gandhi."

Gandhi: (holding his hands in prayer) "May the blessings of Brahma be with you all. And to you Linda, my child, may peace be with you always."

Linda: "Oh, thank you Mahatma—you're so sweet. Next to the Mahatma is the very funny Lucille Ball. Welcome Lucy!"

Lucille: (waving to audience) "Hi everybody! I'm so happy to be here on Linda's show. I watch it all the time and love it. (touching Linda) Linda dear, I especially loved your show with Barbara Streisand. You got along like sisters."

Linda: "Oh, oh—you are so thoughtful—so sweet Lucy. Your remarks about Barbara and me are so true. I- I think I'm going to be verkempt. I'll try to get hold of myself. (waves outstretched palms in a circle) Talk among yourselves. Discuss the difference between pantheism and naturalism."

Lucille: "Don't be silly Linda. I'll take over for a while. You relax. Next to me is the former dictator of Germany Adolf Hitler. How are you doing Adolf?"

Hitler: "*Guten Morgen, meine freunde* in TV land. (waving his index finger) Lucille, *du dummkoph du*, do not use my first name. Call me Herr Hilter!"

Linda" I'm back. My verkempt is over. Thanks Lucille for stepping in. Now, my darlings—my viewers would love to hear about your interests. What is your favorite food. Mine is a bagel—I love them all but my favorite is a blueberry bagel. That and some cream cheese makes me one happy lady. What about yours Mr. President?"

F.D.R.: "Linda, I love pigs feet. At Hyde Park when I was growing up a delicious plate of bigs feet was always served at least once every month."

Linda: "Lucy, do you have a favorite?"

Lucille: "Sure, my favorite is pallela which is seasoned rice with chicken. Desi taught me how to make it. He always added hot peppers to the recipe—which made hot Latin men like Desi even hotter if you know what I mean.""

Linda: "Oh yes Lucy. And did you like that?"

Lucille: "You bettcha! It was like getting a pinata after a meal."

Linda: "Herr Hitler, what is your favorite?"

Hitler: "Since I'm a vegetarian, I do not eat any type of meat. However, I love pastries. My favorite is *sachetorte* which is a rich cake with whip cream. Eva and I had it all of the time. She loved to take the whipped cream and spread it over my mustache before she..."

Linda: "Please, please Herr Hitler. Keep it to yourself. You naughty boy."

Gandhi: "Oh, Brahma, please lead Herr Hitler to the path of righteousness."

Hitler: "Oh, shut up!"

F.D.R. "Oh, I love it. I love it. I can't wait to tell the gang back at the White House about this."

Linda: "What about you dear Mahatma?"

Gandhi: "Linda, my child, I'm a vegetarian too but I do not like sweets. I am very happy with a plate of steamed vegetables and a little rice. It is light on the stomach and doesn't cloud the mind so that one can meditate and seek spiritual enlightenment."

Linda: "Sarah, What is your favorite?"

Sarah: "I do not eat much of anything. I am very conscious of maintaining my lovely figure."

F.D.R.: "And a nice figure it is too!"

Sarah: "*Merci* Mr. President. I think so too. Well, to get back to Linda's question. I do enjoy *crepe suzettes* on rare occasions. That with some campagne makes for a delightful snack."

Linda: "My viewers would like to know who is your favorite performer. Mine is as you know Barbara Streisand. Oh! Oh!—I'm getting verkempt. (waves her outstretched palms in a circle) Talk among yourselves. Discuss Jazz and its connection with philosophy."

Lucille: "Now, now Linda. I'll take over again while you get control of your emotions. My favorite is Charlie Chaplin. I learned how to do pantomine from him. I love to dress up like him or Harpo Marx and do funny routines. Of course, with the Harpo take-off I add a horn. Mr. President, what about you?

F.D.R.: "Well, my friends, my favorite performer is Myrna Loy. She has such wit and class. I think that she did her best work in the Thin Man series."

Linda: "I'm back. Thanks Lucy. Well, what about you Herr Hitler. Do you have a favorite performer?"

Hitler: "*Ja*. I love Marlene Dietrich—although she does not love me. I invited her back to Germany to star in German films. We Germans love her Aryan looks and her lovely voice. But, she told me—and the German people—to go jump in the Rhine. She is a very mischievious lady who deserves a spanking with a...."

Linda: "Stop Herr Hitler. Please! Please! Remember this is a family show."

Sarah: "*Oui*, Herr Hilter—you nasty man—put a lid on it—or as they now say 'cool it.'" I'm sure that Marlene had her reasons. Getting back to the question, my favorite performer is *Moi*—the Divine Sarah. Audiences throughout the world have adored my acting. I have even played Hamlet to rave reviews. How many actresses can do that?"

F.D.R.: "Oh, Divine One, you are right. Even at sixty- five you were a sensation. I remember when you played Joan of Arc at the Barrymore Threatre. In the trial scene when the judge asked you how old you were, you answered—-"(he gestures to Sarah to supply the answer).

Sarah: "'Nineteen!' *Oui!* And everyone stood up and cheered. *Oui*, I remember it with pride. I looked young and beautiful."

F.D.R.: "Tell us Sarah—How did you do it?"

Sarah: "*Mon cher*, it was a matter of make up, lighting and the best corset money could buy. But it was worth it. I looked fabulous."

F.D.R. "And you still do. *Viva* Sarah!"

Linda: "Dear Mahatma, do you have a favorite performer?"

Gandhi: "Well, yes. I love to hear a good zitar player. I find that the sound helps me to achieve spiritual peace and joy."

Linda: "Now, I want to ask you to share your most embarrassing moment with our viewers. Can we start with you dear Mahatma?"

Gandhi: "Well, I have to admit that I was embarrassed when a western photographer found me in bed with three young virgins. She didn't know that I like to resist sexual temptation. It gives me great satisfaction to know that I have mastered my sexual and carnal desires. Besides, I find that the bodies of sweet young girls keep me warm during the cold months."

F.D.R.: "I love it! That's the way to go Gandhi! I love it! I can't wait to tell Eleanor about this. She will not believe it of the Great Soul."

Linda: "What about you Mr. President?"

F.D.R.: "Well, I found one situation more funny that embarrassing. As I was going to the podium at the Democratic Convention in 1936—with my speech in hand—I suddenly found my left leg brace snapping out of place. Of course, I then fell into the laps of several startled delegates. Well, the guys from the secret service picked me up like a sack of potatoes and locked my brace back in place. Jimmy—that's one of my sons—picked up the papers with my speech on it—and I was on my way."

Linda: "Oh, *mon cher*, that must have been very difficult for you."

F.D.R.: "Well, yes—but I had learned to pick myself up and make the best of it. Once in 1929 before I was President I fell on my face in lobby. I used my arms to pull myself over to some stairs so I could grab hold of the railing to pull myself up again. I just smiled all the time while several bystanders stood around looking. I kept saying, 'Oh, this happens a lot. It is nothing to worry about.'"

Sarah: "Bravo Mr. President! Bravo! I know what you mean. After my leg was amputated, I found myself losing my balance and falling at times. But, like you, I put a laugh into the situation and everything worked out."

Linda: "What about you Lucy?"

Lucille: "Once on the **I Love Lucy** show my long fake nose caught on fire. I was doing a skit with William Holden and he accidentally set it on fire with a cigarette lighter that he used to light my cigarette. As I recall, my eyebrows and hair were both singed. However, the stunt got a big laugh which made me feel better. You know, I'll do anything for a laugh."

Linda: "I know, I know. You're one funny lady Lucy."

Linda: "Herr Hitler, what about you?"

Hitler: "Well, it is something like Gandhi's story but in my case a S.S. guard came in unexpectedly and found me whipping Eva Braun's bear bottom. It was hilarious. Eva was laughing and...."

Linda: "Please Herr Hitler—you naughty boy!"

Gandhi: "Oh, Brahma, purify Herr Hitler's heart and guide him to the paths of righteousness. Oh, define Brahma..."

Hitler: "Oh, shut up *du dummkoph du!*

F.D.R.: "I love it! I love it! Wait till Eleanor hears this!"

Linda: "Well, we are running out of time. I was going to ask you about your favorite song."

Sarah: "Oh, let me sing mine to you." (Sarah stands up while she holds on to the table and starts singing) *"Allons, Enfants de La Patrie..."*

Hitler: *"Nein! Nein!"* (Hitler immediately gets up and starts singing loudly)

"Deutchland, Deutchland Ober Alles..."

Linda: "Please, please, let us keep this peaceful. Oh, no, I—I think I am going to get verkempt! I- I am verkempt!"

F.D.R. "I love it! I love it!"

Lucille: "This is Lucille Ball filling in for Linda who is verkempt. (waving her right hand) Goodbye! Goodbye for Coffee Talk!"

INTERVIEW

What is your name?

> Ned Doggybag

What gives you a belly laugh?

> Well, this is embarrassing. I laugh at people who fart. I'll tell you the truth, every time I see Blazing Saddles, I I start belly laughing.

Oh, you don't have to be embarrassed about that. I love that film too.

Do you have a limerick to give us a laugh?

> Sure do.

> > There is a fellow
> >
> > > named Doggybag
> >
> > who was teased that
> >
> > > he carried a
> >
> > large handbag.
> >
> > But he needed a large
> >
> > > bag because he had
> >
> > so many records and memos.
> >
> > He finally got a computer
> >
> > > so he could store all
> >
> > > of his records on a
> >
> > disk which was then stored in his
> >
> > > Appel bag.

Why I Enjoy Collecting Sayings From Church Signs

In the past six years I have been collecting sayings from church signs. I especially like the ones that are funny, clever and insightful. Each says a lot about the author of the sign and the religious denomination that he/she represents. Generally, I have found that the Southern Baptists and the members of the Assemblies of God are the more orthodox, conservative and less funny. The Presbyterians, Lutherans and Catholics are more clever and with it. Some of the best ones have come from Saint Dominic Savio in Affton, Gethsemane Lutheran in St. Louis and the Affton Presbyterian Church.

I have divided my collection into various categories. I'm going to start with the category that I call "offers of help/ reaching out to others." Here are some of the better ones in my collection:

> Tough Week? We're Open Sundays. Come In For A Free Faith Lift.
> We Hold A Family Reunion Every Sunday And You're Invited.
> Soul Food Served Here. Fresh Every Week.
> Do Come In. Tresspassers Will Be Forgiven.

While all of these sound inviting, I wonder if one would really find a welcome. So often the author is hoping that the congregation will be friendly to outsiders. The reality may be very different. A friend of mine went to the church with the second saying out front and received a rather cool reception. So, these sayings may sound good but often they arouse expectations in the minds of those seeking help and friendship that can't be met.

Another category is what I call "adages." They could have come from the pen of Ben Franklin. Here are a few:

Mud Thrown is Ground Lost.

An Ounce of Practice Is Worth A Pound of Preaching.

Don't Open A Can of Worms Unless You Like Worms.

Another category is what I term "advice." Here are some of the better ones in my collection:

If You Fish For Compliments, Don't Be Surprised If You are Handed A Line.

Stand For Something Or You'll Fall For Anything.

If You Don't Know Where You Are Going, You May Miss It When You Get There.

I found a few sayings that fit into the category of "religious wrath." Here are a few:

Here Lies An Atheist All Dressed Up And No Place To Go.

If You Continue To Use My Name In Vain, I'll Make the Rush Hour Longer. God

Well, Darwin—Do You Believe Us Now?

On the other hand I have found many sayings that are good messages for everyone to remember. Here are some of them:

Live Simply That Others May Simply Live.

If You Can Brighten Another Person's Day Do It.

An Apology Is A good Way To Have The Last Word.

Faith Sees God's Face In Every Human Race.

I found that a few churches like to connect up a message with the "season." Here are a few in that category:

Lent Is Spring Cleaning For Christians.
Spring Is God Saying: "One More Time."
Smile. We Know Of Hotter Places.
Prayer Conditioning On The Inside.

Some religious leaders really want to show that they are with it. They take advantage of some current event to bring attention to themselves. Here are some of the better ones in the "current events" category:

Still Don't Believe In Miracles? What About the Rams Winning the Super Bowl?
Even Blockheads Need Love. Thanks For The Insights Charles Schultz.
I'm O.K. U R O.K. In Y2K C U Sunday.
God Calls Upon You By Name. The Government Sends You A Census Form.
There Are No Skyboxes in Heaven. Everyone Is Equal.
God Doesn't Make Political Promises.

Many sayings on the signs have to do with "insights into the human condition." Here are a few of the better ones:

It Is Easier To Crack A Safe Than To Crack A Closed Mind.
There Is More To Life Than Increasing Its Speed.
People Need Love Especially When They Don't Deserve It.

A lot of churches like to have something clever in connection with holidays. Here are a few such sayings:

At The First Fireworks God Said, "Let There Be Light!"

God Rested On The 7th Day. Happy Labor Day!

Top of the Morning To You! You Are Entering A No Blarney Zone.

Give a Hug As A Christmas Gift. One Size Fits All.

Only Turkeys Don't Thank God On Thanksgiving Day.

I have often wondered if using the sayings make a difference in church attendance. I have never seen a study about it. I guess if the sayings really reflect a friendly spirit within the church, sayings like some of the above may have an impact. I have often wanted to meet the people who make up the sayings. I suppose some get them from lists that have been circulating for years. On the other hand some of the sayings seem very original. Also, I wonder if the originator is reflecting the true views of his/ her congregation or simply engaged in wishful thinking. Who knows? It really doesn't matter. I'll continue to add to my collection anyway just because I find so many of the sayings funny and often insightful.

INTERVIEW

What is your name?

    Joyce Flush

What gives you a giggle?

Well, it is very personal. It's when a man kisses me on my neck and blows into my ear.

Well, I understand why you would giggle when that happens.

Do you have a cute limerick for us?

Of course.

    There is a lady
        named Flush
    who was very modest
        and would always
    blush whenever a man
        came close.
    Then all that changed
        when Ted Bush
    came into her life.
    He was so good looking
        and so caring
    that she didn't blush
        when he gently
    dipped her while they
        danced the tango.

"My Funny Valentine"

I couldn't help thinking of the lyrics of **My Funny Valentine** when I looked over the valentines that I received at a February meeting of my Eastern Star Chapter. So many of them were not only sweet but downright funny.

My wife, the Worthy Matron, had told everyone to prepare for an old-fashioned valentine exchange party like we used to have as grade school children. I'm sure you all remember buying or making valentines to exchange at school. It was a lot of fun. There was always a specially decorated box in which to put them. Then, on the special day, students would bring treats for everyone and the cards would be delivered.

As Norma, our organist, played such old-time songs such as **I Can't Give You Anything But Love, I'm in the Mood for Love, and That's Amore** we exchanged cards at Star. I received a wide assortment of them.

Some members had made their cards. I received one that was made using a paper lace heart. Then the sender had glued onto the front a small heart-shaped lollipop and a small valentine. Inside was a picture of a cute male mouse dressed up like an artist and he had painted in a heart these words, "Valentine, you are a work of art!"

Another home made card was a large heart cut out of red construction paper. The sender had taken a seal featuring a bear and donkey embracing and then had written at the top, "Happy Valentine's Day." Still another was made with several small red hearts cut from construction paper and then glued to white note paper. Written inside the hearts were these greetings, "To a special someone—You! A Great Worthy Patron. Happy Valentine's Day!"

An unusual home made valentine was one made to look like a red rose bud. The sender had made a green stem and had attached artificial leaves to it. Then she had taken chocolate kisses and had wrapped them in red tinfoil and had created a rose bud out of them. She even had taken several strings of small pearls to attach behind the rose bud to make it seem that baby's breath had been used. She attached a greeting card to the stem. Inside I found a bear pulling a cart loaded with jars of honey. The bear was telling me: "Happy Valentin's Day. Bee my valentine!"

I received a lot of small cards featuring a dalmatian puppy saying the following funny messages: "Happy Valentine's Day to a spotacular friend!"; "I can spot a friend a mile away!"; "Just barking a big Happy Valentine's Day your way!"; "Have a doggone happy Valentine's Day!"; "Have the best pawssible Valentines Day!" They were all so cute and clever.

There were many cards featuring Snoopy and often his little bird friend Woodstock. The following were unusually sweet and funny:

> Snoopy looking at a crystal ball says, "Snoopy sees all, knows all! He predicts you'll be my valentine!"
> Snoopy jumping up and down says, "I'd jump for joy if you'd be my valentine!"

Many had Snoopy embracing Woodstock and saying the following:

> "You're fun to hang out with!"; "It's so nice to have a friend like you!"
> One featured Woodstock by himself saying, """""That's bird talk for Happy Valentine's Day!"

I received several cards featuring a smiling bear with a happy go-lucky piglet. The following greating appeared:

> "Two is friendier than one on Valentine's day!"; "A very, very grand Valentine's Day to you!"
> Some cards featured Walt Disney cartoon characters. On one Snow White is saying to Grumpy, "I'll be grumpy if you won't be my valentine!" Another showed Minne Mouse sipping a soda and saying, "Thinking sweet thoughts of you on Valentine's Day!"

Finally, there were a few cards featuring other animals or birds. One had a red parrot saying, "If you won't be my valentine—waddle I do?" Another had a sad bulldog saying, "No drippy, mushy goo—just happy Valentine's Day to you!"

As I look over all these cards, I feel that special joy of a grade school child on Valentine's Day and find myself smiling and laughing at the funny cards. So, no wonder I'm singing to myself the words to **My Funny Valentine:**

> "My funny valentine, Sweet comic valentine,
> you make me smile with my heart.
> —Your looks are laughable, unphotograph-ble,
> yet, you're my favorite work of art.
> Is your figure less than Greek; is your mouth a little weak,
> when you open it to speak, are you smart?
> —But don't change a hair for me,
> not if you care for me, stay little valentine stay!
> Each day is Valentine's Day."

INTERVIEW

What is your name?

    Mark Cookie

What makes you laugh?

    When my wife teases me and tickles me on my butt.

Well, I understand. Do you have a limerick to share?

    Yes. Here goes.

        There is a guy named

           Cookie

      who can do more than

          eat cookies.

      He likes to chase all

          the girls

    to get some

          nukkie.

      But a cutie came along

          who refused to

      give him any nukkie.

    So, he went back to

          eating cookies

      rather than being locked up

          in a jailie.

Funny Greetings on St. Patrick's Day

This year I find myself looking forward to celebrating St. Patrick's Day. For years the thought of wearing green, planning a St. Pat's party and sending out greeting cards to mark the day were not to my liking. Why? Because of all the violence in Northern Ireland. It had really turned me against things Irish. In fact, there for awhile I took pride in the fact that all my people came from England. I began to think that all the Irish were bull-headed, intolerant and violent.

But, since things have quieted down in Ireland, I have regained some of my enthusiasm for St. Patrick's Day and the Irish in general.

Recently, I even went to the store and purchased greeting cards to send to friends to celebrate the day and spread Irish cheer.

I found that many of the cards were very sentimental. The following greeting was especially sentimental about all things Irish:

> "May you feel sweet Irish breezes
> blowing across your face;
> May Irish music now be heard
> lilting through your place;
> May all your days be filled up
> to the brim with Irish cheer;
> And may the good Lord bless you
> and hold you dear."

I also found many that were very light-hearted and down right funny. There were several that featured funny questions. Here are two of them:

"What's Irish and sits in the backyard all night?" The answer is found inside the card. "Why, it's Paddy O'Furniture!"

"What do you call those small green buildings inhabited by Irish wee folk?" Inside the card one reads: "Leprecondos!"

Other cards featured amusing observations about Irish symbols. Here are a few of them:

"The Irish must be one of the most passionate peoples in the world."

The explanation is inside the card. "Because they are willing to stand in line to kiss a stone."

"It's St. Patrick's Day! So, get out there and shake your shamrocks!"

"It's a family tradition to run around town on St. Pat's with a big shamrock painted on your chest!

That Grandma—What a fun-loving nut!"

"This card contains a personal message from the tiny leprechauns in the enchanted forest. Send tiny women, please!"

If one of your friends has a birthday that falls on St. Pat's day, you can send one of these special cards to him or her:

"In your honor on St. Patrick's Day a shamrock has been planted in Ireland. (Your day to water—Wednesdays)" Happy Birthday!

"To share this big day with St. Pat is grand fun, and better yet, it's about as close to sainthood as ye'll probably ever get! Happy Birthday!"

To all of you here I send you this greeting on St. Pat's Day:

"Three cheers for the Irish!
O' Hip, Hip, Hooray!
The Irish all year
And the Irish today!
Three cheers for the Irish!
And after that's through,
Three rousing cheers more
For wonderful you!"

Happy St. Patrick's Day!

INTERVIEW

What is your name?

  Coke Popcorn

What makes you chuckle?

  Seeing the butt of a gorgeous gal shake.

Oh my! I bet you have a limerick for us.

I sure do.

    There was a cowpoke

      named Coke

   who loved horses

     more than a

   fast poke with some

      SALOON GAL.

   That all changed when

     Lilly came along.

   Lilly was a lady who

     could ride side saddle

  on any horse in the county.

  So, one day Coke proposed

     to Lilly

  so that they could ride

     together not only

  in the bedroom but on

  the open range.

How To Gain Instant Popularity

1. Dogs growl and bark at me. yes no
2. Cats hiss and arch their backs when they see me. yes no
3. Children hide behind their parents when they see me. yes no
4. People make a fast exit when they see me. yes no
5. People refuse to vote for me even for insignificant offices such as door keeper. yes no
6. People refuse my offer to give them a lift even though they need a ride. yes no
7. People refuse my offer to loan them money despite the fact that they really need the cash. yes no
8. People refuse to dine with me in spite of the fact that I offer to pick up the tab including the tip for the waiter. yes no
9. People refuse my offers of help in emergencies. yes no
10. Behind my back people refer to me as "the Grinch." yes no

Now score yourself to see how much people like or dislike you. Give yourself 5 points for each "no" answer.

50 points—People think you are the greatest.

45-40 points—People like you a lot.

35-30 points—People tolerate you.

25-20 points—People really dislike you.

15-10 points—People hate and despise you.

If your score was 35 points or below, you need my service—and the sooner the better.

Well, here it is—the solution that will give you instant popularity: dress up as Santa Claus.

My wife and I can testify to the immediate popularity of dressing up like the most popular elf on the planet. Believe us when we say, "Everyone adores Santa."

As proof let me tell you about some of the most memorable reactions to my becoming the ever popular Santa Claus.

Once I walked around my neighborhood dressed as the dear old elf. When I reached the main road outside our subdivision, I started waving at the passing cars. Well, the people in the cars went crazy—they waved back, and tooted their horns. Many lowered their windows and shouted, "Hello Santa" or "We love you Santa."

Another time I dressed as Santa to hand out present to children. My wife who was dressed as Mrs. Santa and I had to drive to Centralia, Illinois to make the deliveries. As we drove down the highway, drivers waved and tooted their horns. When we got to Centralia, we were greeted with smiles and waves at every stop sign or red traffic light. Everytime we had to stop at an intersection, the people walking along the sidewalks would first get that suprised look—then the realization that they were really seeing Mr. and Mrs. Santa Claus—and then they would start smiling and waving automatically as if they were greeting their most beloved relatives.

Finally, another time I dressed as Santa to go to a nursing home to visit the residents there. I had been there before as myself. Usually the residents would seem off in their own little worlds or so drugged that they were out of it. Well, when I appeared as Santa, every resident came alive. They knew Santa alright. They usually said things like, "Hello Santa" or "I love you Santa." One little lady started crying for joy and exclaimed, "Santa, I thought you would never come." Naturally, every one of them wanted a picture taken with Santa.

Now, if you are going to embrace this solution, you have to go about it in the right way. Here are guidelines to ensure instant popularity as Santa:

1. Be sure to get a terrific looking Santa outfit. It will be expensive but consider it an investment. You need all the help you can get to shake the "Grinch" image that you have.

2. Get a good make-up artist to do your face so that you really look old but jolly. Be sure to buy a curley white beard and a whig that look like the real things.

3. If you need some padding to look chubby, use the best foam rubber you can get.

4. Practice Santa's belly laugh a lot. When he goes "Ho Ho Ho!" he holds his sides and rocks back and forth.

5. Practice Santa's movements in front of a mirror. Be sure to master his wave, his walk and especially what he does as he gives out with a jolly belly laugh.

6. Practice saying phrases associated with Santa such as: "Have a holly jolly Christmas" and "Come Dancer, Come Vixen, Come Comet and Blitzen" and "Have you been a good little boy (or girl)?" and "Merry Christmas to all and to all a good night."

7. Practice holding a bag filled with toys and presents. This may require some work with weights at a gym.

8. Get used to drinking lots of cocoa and eggnog and eating cookies so you will be prepared for all the goodies that you will be given by children.

9. Be sure to buy a string of jingle bells to carry with you.

10. Pick up some dog biscuits and kitty treats (some catnip is highly recommended) to take with you. Practice talking kindly to animals. Knell down when you talk to them. Be prepared to rub tummies and to pet heads and to say, "Oh, you are such a wonderful little dog or cat."

11. Buy some CD's with happy Santa Claus songs, such as "Here Comes Santa Claus" and "Jolly Old Saint Nicholas." As you listen to the songs, sing along. It will help you capture the jolly spirit of Santa.

12. Be sure to know all the names of Santa's reindeer and elfs along with other information about Santa's home at the North Pole. Remember that little children are sharp when it comes to knowledge about Santa Claus.

As part of our service, we will assist in your training and attend your practice sessions and hold a final dress rehearsal.

Now you are probably wondering how much this will cost you. Well, we expect the following: twelve drummers drumming, eleven pipers piping, ten lords a-leaping, nine ladies dancing, eight maids a-milking, seven swans-a-swimming, six geese a-laying, five gold rings, four calling birds, three French hens, two turtle doves, and a partridge in a pear tree.

Naturally, you can pay for our services on the installment plan.

Oh, there is one other thing that I want to tell you about. Really it is a warning. You will find like I did that the power of Santa can be awesome. You will find yourself being pursued by hundreds of fans. You will find that animals will not stop licking your face. You will find that everyone will want either your autograph or your picture or both. However, you will find in time that you will adjust to this tremendous popularity. Keep reminding yourself that it is certainly a lot better than being treated liked the Grinch.

INTERVIEW

What is your name?

 Minnie Wennie

What makes you laugh?

 See comics do things in unison—like dancing.

I like to laugh at that too. I love physical humor.

Do you have a limerick to share?

I'll try. It may not be as funny as some. Here goes.

 There is a girl

  named Minnie

 who never could tolerate

  seeing a man's

  wennie.

 She is a shy and

  bashful girl.

 She believes that sexy

  things should be

  corralled.

 She wants a guy to be

  attentive and

 loving before he pulls out

  his wennie

 to give a good time to

  Minnie.

Holiday Sights and Sounds

A few weeks ago I was sorting through our collection of video cassettes.

I discovered that we had purchased or taped from TV at least 20 holiday offerings.

We have the entire Charlie Brown series—the "Great Pumpkin" through Thanksgiving, Christmas, New Year's, Valentine's Day and Easter.

I decided to make a project of viewing our Christmas collection. I started with Charles Dickens' *A Christmas Carol.*

From the library I got the audio cassette of the story as narrated by Sir John Gielgud.

I had read the story every year while I still could read a book. I fact, I can recite the narrative along with the reader.

One year I read it to our three Chihuahuas, hoping that bossy Cleopatra might learn to become kinder and gentler like Scrooge in the end. Of course, it did not work.

I pulled my chair close to the TV and played the 1951 black-and-white version starring Alastair Sim as Scrooge. This version, while faithful to the book, provides additional background about how the Scrooge-Marley partnership began and why Scrooge became so bitter.

In 1970 a musical version, *Scrooge,* was produced, starring Albert Finney. I remember thinking at the time, "A musical?" But it is delightful. My favorite song from it is "Thank You Very Much," sung by the soup vendor Tom Jenkins while dancing on Scrooge's coffin. Scrooge, meanwhile, is perplexed and wonders who is being thanked for dying.

Then come the less serious versions.

The Muppet Christmas Carol stars Michael Caine, with a cast of hundreds of cute little Muppet characters. Gonzo narrates. Kermit the Frog plays Bob Crachit, and who else but Miss Piggy to play his wife? The sons look like their father and the daughters like their mother.

I wonder what Dickens would have thought of a frog saying, "God bless us everyone!"

Marley becomes the Marley brothers, Jacob and Robert. Old Fezziwig—I just love the names Dickens created for his characters throughout his books—becomes a dealer in rubber chickens.

Scrooge McDuck played Scrooge in the Mickey Mouse version and the Nearsighted Mr. Magoo also had his version.

The most hilarious version, however, is *Blackadder's Christmas Carol,* or how to have a mucked up Christmas.

In a reversal of the story, Ebenezer Blackadder is a sweet, generous man at the start. By the end he has become as mean as the original Scrooge. Christmas Past takes place in the Elizabethan Era, complete with the appearance of the old girl herself. Christmas Yet to Come takes place in a futuristic space station. Christmas Present features a zany Queen Victoria and a bumbling Prince Albert. Even Lord Nelson gets in on the act. You really have to see this to believe it.

After my romp with Mr. Dickens, I was off to visit Rudolf, Frosty, the Grinch and the rest of the cartoon gang.

I relived the Macy's Thanksgiving Day Parade through both the black-and-white and color remake of *Miracle on 34th Street.*

I completed my video tour with the tape of Handel's *Messiah* made in 1996, when I sang with the Community Choral Society of SIU-Edwardsville. This had been the realization of a dream for me, and it brought back many pleasant memories.

Seeing all of these videos put me in the holiday spirit. They helped me recapture the sights and sounds of the season.

In Memorial

To all the members of my writing group that have gone off to join Peter Pan to spread joy to those who need smiles, giggles and belly laughs.

There once was a fellow called Bud
When wounded bled ink 'stead of blood
Each Wednesday at ten
He'd whip out his pen
And let words come out like a flood.

There once was a lady named Cole
Who loved to plant plants in a hole
She'd water and weed
And coax each little seed
And end up with blooms to extol.

There once was a lady, Louise
Who turned out prose with great ease
In German and English
Complete without anguish
And all she surely did please.

There once was a man named Ed
Who lived and loved to be wed
Seems that was his style
He'd say with a smile
And tell all with a shake of his head.

There once was a lady called Jake
Who left many a swain in her wake
By the wayside they'd fall
As she toasted them all
With Dom Perignon for their sake.

There once was a gal named Lucille
Who wrote lyrical verse with appeal
While sailing the seas
To the sound of a breeze
Or at home where she scribbled with zeal.

Buddy Webb

There once was a lady named Kelly
By no means a Machiavelli
Its children she loves
And treats with kid gloves
To her smile and wit sweet as jelly.

There once was a lady named Betty
Who spun plots like bubbling spaghetti
Tongue in cheek she would write
Of a knave or a knight
And served up Poirot Cappeletti.

There once was a lass called Dwyer
Who wrote with vigor and fire
With her cats by her side
She'd damn or deride
Any fool who was lacking desire.

There once was a lady named Pat
Who donned a word-wizard's hat
To weave a fustian mystique
Thru pun or pithy critique
Just to see what you'd think of all that.

Au Revoir! Adjo! Addio.!

BONA SERA! GOOD-BYE! AUF WIEDERSEHEN!

Well, that's all there is folks! I hope that your journey through all the silly pieces and sketches have given you many smiles, giggles and perhaps a few belly laughs.

Close friendship with a friend
brings smiles and happiness.

About the Author

Buddy Webb was born in Germany and was brought to this country after the Night of the Broken Glass in 1938.

He grew up in Moline, Illinois and earned a B.A. from Augustana College and a M.A. in history from the University of Illinois.

He taught social studies for thirty-three years, mainly at Webster Groves High School in St. Louis County.

In retirement he became interested in creative writing.

He has published the folowing books: Echoes and Shadows of Life, Nights of the Black Moon and Days of Sunshine, Dreams, Wishes and Fantasies of Common Folk and Home Front Diary—1944—A Family's Awakening to Truth and Courage.

In retirement he also became a stand-up comic in some of the "joints" and "dives" in the greater St. Louis area. His stage name was Buddy Alley. Under that pen name Author House published his book Zany Humor for Elves, Imps and Clowns.

Xlibris published another humorous book that he wrote entitled "Dear Penis, My Love!": A Hilarious Study of a Penis Obsession under the pen name of Louise Webb. In it he writes funny take offs of the classics—everything from plays by Shakespeare to poems by Chaucer.

Buddy Webb as Buddy Alley
doing a gig at a local St. Louis "dive."

Printed in the United States
By Bookmasters